CW01475385

Horsemanship

Myth Magic and Mayhem

Holly Davis

DEDICATION

For all of the horses and people that are seeking a
better way forwards.

For my own horses - both past and present.

For the horses and people that have come into
my life
and created positive change and thought.

With much love and gratitude for all horses.
Whoever and wherever they may be.

ACKNOWLEGMENTS

Cover Photograph
Tim Duckworth at Bitless and Barefoot
From the Arabian Nights Collection

Photographs
Elenore Bowden-Bird
Kathryn Hulland

Foreword
Sue Gardner
Human & Horse Trainer
Author of Applied Equine Behaviour Home
Study Courses

CONTENT

FOREWORD

Holly truly does get to the heart of the matter. This book delivers far more than you could imagine and way more than the title. No stone is left unturned whilst Holly shares with us her insights and her wealth of knowledge. Holly's philosophy is very grounded and based on positive ethical and practical ways to best understand and live in harmony with horses. Holly has the perfect web address Centaur Horsemanship because this is the ultimate goal. To truly have a Centaur Relationship.

Holly is concerned with the heart and the soul of horsemanship that is the horse and human connection. She shares ways to get us to think outside the box (excuse the pun). We are asked to be mindful, really mindful! to consider our horses in ways that we might not have normally given ourselves time to consider let alone accomplish.

Holly asks us to consider not only their innate needs but their unique personality and therefore their strengths and weakness as well as their desires. Each horse is motivated in a different way; do we truly know our horse and his needs outside of the fundamental food shelter and safety? Can we be an interesting and imaginative partner and friend, are we positively enhancing our horses natural gifts or simply frustrating them by not even recognising their strengths.

The amount and depth of information Holly has shared in this book will benefit horses and humans everywhere. Much more than Myth Magic and Mayhem, Holly provides insightful information on why things go wrong (part of The Mayhem) and then shares how to put them right, whether that be transporting or working in liberty, ground skills and ridden (part of The Magic). When I say no stone is left un-turned I mean it, she seems to have covered huge areas including nutrition too!

So, without wishing to take too much of the magic from the book by putting it into the foreword I will summarise it in this one statement that Holly makes because it is such a powerful truth.

"We have a choice; a choice to feel or not to feel the horse. When we deny ourselves and our horse this sacred connection, never can we expect to have the depth of trust and knowing that so many of us say we have been seeking"

I will pray for that Holly......... Amen.........
Namaste ......

Foreword by Sue Gardner
Human & Horse Trainer - Author of Applied Equine Behaviour Home Study Courses

Sue has been working in the field of equine partnerships for 45 years. She had her first pony when she was 9 and her first herd of horses aged only 13. Sue was short listed for the Prince Philip Cup and was competing in show jumping and cross country as well as handling the foals bred on the family property. By being able to observe herd behaviour and by having a horse whisperer as a neighbour (not that they were called that in 1969!) Sue had an opportunity to develop what was innately within her.

Sue had a way of helping horses who had become troubled and her ability and reputation soon spread; horses were being sent to her even though she was not yet 16, it was the start of her journey to discovering the innate behaviour of horses and how to apply this to ethical welfare and training.

Over her 45 years in the world of horses she has written many articles and run workshops and courses; lectures and demonstrations. Most importantly Sue has helped many hundreds of equines and many hundreds of humans to develop themselves and their equine relationships through gaining a deeper level of understanding and therefore a higher level of confidence and trust.

Sue has put all this knowledge into a theory based home study program in the hope that this will reach far and wide into those homes that are both needing and searching for such knowledge.

Maria Olarte

INTRODUCTION

The word 'horsemanship' can conjure up all kinds of images for an individual in thought.

Horses wide eyed, flying around a round-pen, looking for the next set of instructions from the trainer - to the calm liberated horses seeking solace in the company of the one they look to as their human friend and ally.

During my years of horsemanship, I have studied many methods of training whilst in the company of horses. My work as an Animal Communicator has given me a privileged glimpse into the world of the equine mind, their thoughts, feelings and emotions. The very places so often not visited by the average horse 'owner'.

I use the word 'owner' within this book to describe the person who has bought, or been given the horse; the person with which the horse lives. It in no way implies that we can 'own' a horse. Horses are themselves - we can never 'own' them, other than in the sense of the law and our own limiting mindset.

What I have experienced in the company and presence of horses, I have to say has been life changing - their ability to shift from the wild prey animal that is innate, to the loyal and wise companion. The feelings and emotions they have caused to stir within me, the lessons taught and honoured in the true sense with which they were offered by my four legged friends.

Upon taking on my first horse in my early twenties, life changed. It caused me to question why, we as humans, were feeling the need to control these majestic creatures. Big though they are, they have the ability to be the most gentle animals to ever walk this planet.

They may strike, they may kick and bite, but this is purely circumstantial to their ability to live in the moment and act as needed, given every situation presented to them.

The wild stallion that fights for his mares and the dam that fights to protect her off spring is far removed from our domesticated horses that exhibit such behaviours due to pain, frustration and inability to tolerate the barrage of information. Information that is both false and true being flung at them from all directions by humans.

Should our horse, our loyal companion exhibit any of these behaviours, in fact any behaviour other than relaxed calm and focused calm. We need to look deep inside of not only the horse, but also our selves to enable us to find the cause to be found, so that the issue may be resolved.

So many times we hear of horses being referred to as, naughty, nasty, grumpy, dominant....

Horses will not be any of these things without a valid reason for doing so. Are they really these negative descriptions we place upon their heads? If any of these traits are seen within the general personality or indeed periodically, there is a cause that needs to be found. The displaying of such a trait or emotion is not truly the horse. Rather, it is an energetic form of information carrier presented to you, by the horse, in physical format. It is the horse's wish that you read these signs and the message behind them. Sometimes this message is about them themselves, whilst other times it is about us. It is our job as owner and caretaker to work out which and resolve the underlying issues, regardless of who they originate from.

Sadly so many horses are punished for their behaviour - owners, riders and trainers failing the horse over and over by not enquiring of them, the cause of their behaviour.

During these times do we really think that the horse has no cause?

No feeling other than to portray a behaviour or trait that we as an owner consider undesirable?

Do we really think that such behaviour is of benefit to our horse other than to annoy us?

The sad truth is that millions of horses in domestication, on a daily basis have to face indiscriminate torture from humans. This is due to the human's inability to read and view them as sentient, living breathing beings, each with their own life path, individual personalities, needs and desires. As a species we have sadly let down these horses that have come to teach us and have offered us lessons and insights. All too often these offerings have been allowed to fall upon deaf ears, due to our own ignorance and lack of seeking our own knowledge.

So many hearts still remain closed; our eyes limited to what we want to see. Ears and minds closed to the horses that scream and the horses that weep.

In recent years it has become apparent that the divide between the working and natural horse worlds has become greater. By this I mean that the cruelty that should be condemned to the history books is still flourishing, sadly even more so in some ways than it has in the past. The cruelty of Rollkur and the Tennessee Walking Horses are just two examples. And yet - we are in a time of a new generation of horse people, those who are waking up to the truth of the horse - their thirst for knowledge and their enquiring minds wide open. They are following guidance from the horses themselves, the true teachers of horsemanship, to engulf their hearts and minds. New understandings come as the horses enable the stripping away of our outdated rigid mindsets that have held us back all these years as a race.

When we choose to make dominant decisions over the lives of our horses, we take from them their ability to make choices - these same choices that enable them to grow and learn as an individual. In turn we deprive ourselves of the unique gift that every minute in the presence of the horse has to offer us.

It is all too easy to stroke a horse - but how many of us can actually 'feel' the horse? By this I am not meaning that we put a hand on their hip or shoulder and can feel the physical structure beneath our palm. I am referring to the inner being of the horse, creating the energetic connection that enables within that moment in time, true connection and 'feel' to be found. It may only last seconds and yet this simple thing - this opening to new realisations is often lost, dismissed and neglected for want of just getting on with riding and grooming our horses.

When true connection is made and has been established, things are never quite the same again. Whilst we may be busy and unable to hold that focus during all of our interactions with our horse, it should never be forgotten. We only have to look deep into our horse's eyes to see the emotion staring right back at us - often reflecting our own.

How can one look into their eyes and not feel touched and have their heart opened?

We have a choice; a choice to feel or not to feel the horse. When we deny ourselves and our horse this sacred connection, never can we expect to have the depth of trust and knowing that so many of us say we have been seeking. The truth is many are scared to feel the horse; scared because it opens up new emotions that can overspill and flood us. As the horse lays us wide open to ourselves and all we are - scary? Yes - but again what these humble horses are offering us within these moments is ourselves in all we are. Why do we have to be scared of ourselves? What is it we are hiding from?

For many, waking up to the horse can be a liberating experience, as indeed it has been for my self. For others it can be hard, guilt over how we have treated our horses over the years and the need to admit we have been wrong can be so hard. Yet hand on heart I think I can truly say that no horse person can say they have got it right all of the time - we have all made mistakes. Over the years I have had many people cry as they tell me what they have done to their horse in the past, and how guilty they feel because of it. I quietly tell them...'Let the guilt go. It only need be felt when we know it is wrong and yet we continue to continue with such negative behaviours'.

But what is most important to a horse?

What is it we have to offer them most to fulfil their inner need?

By this I am not referring to the everyday essentials in life such as food, water and equine companionship. Rather, the innate need that every horse seeks - acknowledgment. Acknowledgment of who they are and even their very existence.

How many of us walk past the stable door, or past our horse in the field, only to focus on our intention of what we are doing rather than our horse? How many of us absent mindedly say 'hello', or give them a pat as we pass? The next time you do this your horse will do one of two things. If you turn as you walk past and see him staring back at you, then he is seeking your acknowledgment that he has experienced before. He is asking you to come back to him. Take a few minutes from your busy schedule and just *be with him* However, if he keeps his head down and carries on grazing without so much as his eyes following you, you can read this as a sure sign that you have failed to acknowledge your horse too many times in the past. He is not even seeking it, as the expectation and hope of that acknowledgment has lapsed over time.

When did you last see your horse? Life is short - things happen. What if the last time you saw them was to be the last time - ever. Hold this thought each time you are with your horse. Not in sadness or paranoia, but as a way of acknowledging that every moment spent with your equine companion is precious and a moment you can never reclaim - savour it. Do not just pass them by. Even thirty seconds can make a difference between a life of acknowledgment and acceptance and a life of feeling invisible.

The hectic life styles that we lead today can often leave us with little time for contemplation and important thoughts. Set yourself a challenge; set aside a little time each day to *be* with your horse. Even if it is only a few minutes, it will make a difference. Stand with them, breathe deeply and slowly and watch for their signs of release. Bring your thoughts to mind; your thoughts of the day. The struggles, the joys and the complex issues you are trying to fathom. As you breathe, relax and allow those feelings to be felt, as your horse shares in those emotions with you. I promise you he will know and feel them too. Clear your mind and allow answers to come to the questions you are asking. These may come as thoughts, words, or even as pictures. However they may present themselves, just honour and acknowledge the spirit in which they were offered to you. Then 'thank' your horse for sharing in this special moment with you - for he has facilitated your healing, as indeed you have in that moment aided his healing too.

THE MYTHS

When we listen to those that engage in horsemanship and training with their horses, all kinds of sayings are associated with the horse and horsemanship by the trainer. By sayings, I am referring to not all sayings, but rather those that carry an element of myth and sometimes also truth within them.

The horse needs a leader

The horse must not invade your space without being invited

The horse must listen to you

You need to keep the horse moving

I am training this horse

The Horse Needs a Leader

Does the horse need a leader? The answer to this question is both 'yes' and 'no'. No doubt there will be some horses that do. To enable me to explain this better I am going to put it into a human context. Our job, our career in life - What do we do? Do we work for a large company where we have to work as a team and within strict guidelines? Do we work under a demanding boss that is also a perfectionist? Or, do we work for ourselves in a vocational role?

When we set out to either find employment or to work for ourselves, the direction in which we search will largely be down to our personality. Like us, all horse personalities are unique. Therefore, each horse will be best suited to a certain type of work, training method and trainer.

The Co Leader

Those of us that have chosen to work for ourselves, will likely find the thought of working a structured nine to five job, under someone else's instruction rather unpalatable. In plain speaking, we like to be our own boss and choose our own structure and not to be tied down and unable to create change where we see it is needed. In horse terms these are the independent horses. The horses that have minds like a sponge and that like to learn and explore. The horses that will listen to what you have to say, think about it and make adaption where needed. It does not mean that they are not respecting what you are asking. Rather, that through their own insight and exploration and willingness to teach those of us that are open to learning. They are just carrying out the role best suited to their personality - one of independence, both teacher and student, and in this instance also truth seeker. The wonderful thing about these horses is that when they are with a like minded trainer, neither steps on the other's toes, or tells each other they are wrong. Instead, they throw about ideas together and when one comes up with an answer, the other in turn will offer other possible solutions. They work together to find the best possible way forwards suited to both parties. This enables them to come to a mutual decision over the desired and best outcome. By doing this there is no clashing of personalities within their work, they are both simply doing things their way, but together. Having found that middle ground and respect for each other's ideas, needs and desires.

These are the horses that are best suited to a trainer of similar traits. A trainer that will question the horse and figure out what is coming back by way of answer from the horse through their behaviour, is likely to be a non dominant person. One that views the horse as their equal and understands that both they and the horse are student and teacher and that by listening to each other, those roles can and do change as the presenting experiences arise.

The Structured Leader

So who are the horses that need leaders? These are the horses that have problems seeking answers to presenting questions - those that are not so much the free thinkers and explorers of life. Rather than just being asked the question, they like to also be given the answer that goes with it. 'This is what I am asking of you and this is how I would like you to reply'. To ask the question of such a horse and leave them searching in the dark for the correct answer, can cause much stress for them. These are the horses that without full instruction feel out on a limb and alone. They are constantly looking to you as the trainer, for answers. When those answers don't come, stress and worry does.

These are the nine to five workers that have their day mapped out for them. They are told what to do and how to do it. Whilst they may not like their job, their job is 'known' and therefore fits safely within their comfort zone. Simply, for these workers - these personalities, often what is not particularly liked but is understood can bring comfort because the answer is known, as is the outcome. Therefore, for the horse there will be no unexpected surprises. These horses like structure and routine. They like you to arrive at the stables at 8am and like you to give them their dinner at 6pm. Any deviation from their routine can be unsettling for them.

The Dominant Leader

Then we have the dominant leaders; those at the top which others must be seen to bow down to, the dominant amongst us, those that will not take 'no' for any answer 'he who must be obeyed'.

At this point I must split the dominant leader into two categories:

Those that have earnt their rightful place because they work from the heart, and those that are self elected dominant leaders - because they work from the ego.

The Inner Strength Heart Leader

The dominant leader that works from the heart, is the leader that works with inner strength and is not therefore truly dominant. The leader that finds it natural and easy to work with stallions and other horses that would see fit to challenge lesser humans, as seen from their perspective. They are firm and fair but take no messing! They adapt themselves well to each individual horse.

Where the horse needs to be met with dominance, or rather 'inner strength' in the disguise of dominance, they can meet them. Such a person that has proved their worth by working from the heart, so as not to let the ego override is, able to meet the dominant horse on their own level. The way they do this is through the heart. Their ability to recognise the dominance within themselves as inner strength is so, in turn, recognised by the horse. This person is truthful and the horse knows this. There is now no challenge to be had - the trainer has earnt their respect.

The Dominant Ego Leader

This person as the title implies, works from their ego. They want to win and come out on top, no matter what the cost. Sadly these types of trainers have an inability to recognise the different personalities within individual horses. Rather than nurture those in need of comfort and meet the dominant stallion on their own level. They choose to dominant all personalities presented to them. They likely treat every horse the same way and stick to the same training techniques, 'one size fits all'. They have an agenda for the outcome they are wanting and will achieve it - no matter what the cost to the horse. Sadly this can cause rise to too much pressure being inflicted on any type of horse personality. There is no middle ground between trainer and horse. Quite simply the trainer is the trainer and the horse is their student that must comply.

These types of leaders can bring great stress to all types of horse personalities. They can wear down the stallion, mentally exhaust and physically impair him. That is of course unless the trainer ends up hospitalised first. The horse in need of structure will incur much anxiety. The instruction and the way in which it is presented is as much a blow to the mental body as it is to their physical. Likely these types of personalities will just shut down, become stoic and just comply through fear.

Dare I say this type of trainer has no business being around horses and interacting with them in any way shape or form. The only one within such training sessions that will 'win' will be the trainer - never the horse. As such a trainer has nothing to offer a horse, other than exhaustion and a confused body, mind and soul. They have no interest in the psychology or the emotion's of the horse. Their only agenda is that of domination and compliance.

The Horse Must Not Invade Your Space Without Being Invited

This is not so much a myth, as a misunderstanding. Unknowingly many people invite their horses into their space only to chastise them for having entered. Everything we do - every breath, thought and movement we make, is information to the horse. Even the information we do not intend to send out as instruction. Upon first meeting a horse, some of us will walk straight up to them and touch them. For some horses this can be very invasive. We have not stopped and asked them first if it is acceptable for us to do so. If the horse is used to having his space invaded and if he is not of a very sensitive personality, he will likely by now, have become used to it and not give any indication that you have been rude. What is the point if in the past the horse has signalled that they have felt invaded and the behaviour from the human has carried on regardless? How many times has he protested only to be ignored? - Leaving him numb to the fact and no longer able to recognise his entitlement to such respect.

If we deem this acceptable on one side of the partnership, then surely it would seem reasonable to the horse that it works both ways? Why is invading their space acceptable and them invading your space not? Surely this is about mutual respect is it not?

We then have the other kind of approach. The one that is respectful to the horse, where we 'ask' to enter their space and wait to be invited in. This in turn teaches the horse that space is indeed a personal thing and that the respect for it needs to work both ways. It is of no use invading our horse's space, whilst at the same time asking them to respect our own. Where is the balance in this? Further more, why would we feel it acceptable to inflict ourselves on our horse and disrespect them in such a way?

Does your horse when he sees you, immediately walk up to you and stick his nose in your face?

If so what is behind this?

Is it actually meant as invasive?

Well that all depends on what the horse is looking to achieve. A fearful horse that sees you as their structured leader will feel safe in your company, making it only natural for them to feel safe in your space. It is not their intention to invade your space, but simply to feel safe within your company. Your job as care giver is to enable them to feel safe in their own space and this is the fundamental lesson from such a horse. It is their request and clue to you, that all is not well in their world and that it needs attending to.

The invasive horse that feels it is acceptable to invade your space may only be doing so as they have not been instructed and told other wise. If we have repeatedly allowed these personalities to invade our space, demanding attention, it is then unfair of us to reprimand them for what we have allowed them to do. Rather, as a way to rectify the situation we must kindly ask them to remove themselves from our space and reward them for doing so. We need to remain consistent in this, or confusion will be created for the horse and frustration for us.

Is your horse just simply offering you a kiss or gentle nuzzle?

If so is this actually invasive?

Or can we liken it to a child that is happy to see us and greets us in a kind and compassionate way?

Do we not like physical contact and to be in the company of those we enjoy?

Next we arrive at the bolshy horse; the horse that likes to invade space and will push into you. Have we invited this behaviour by not saying it is unacceptable? Whatever the cause of this ongoing behaviour it is not in the best interests of your partnership, it does not contain respect. Not respect from the horse towards us, or us respecting ourselves by allowing it to continue.

Again if we have not corrected the horse previously, we are as much to blame for this behaviour as he is, if not more so. In light of this, kind correction is needed and reward offered when the horse removes himself from our personal space.

Sadly all invasive horses are often viewed as just plain bolshy, without the reasons behind the behaviour being considered. This now bring us to the anxious space invader. This horse does not feel safe within his own company; nor does he feel fully safe in yours. When he weighs up the options, he decides that it is better to be eaten by lions with someone else rather than alone. He enters your space in a bid to stop himself feeling as vulnerable as he feels when alone. Sadly the fact that he does not feel safe is the foundation of his apparent bolshy behaviour. Such horses will likely be high head carriers and spend much of their time on red alert. They need the calmness of the Co Leader with the instruction of the Structured Leader. The Dominant Leader would be a fate worse than death for them.

In truth, how we are inwardly will have a dramatic effect on each and every horse that we newly encounter. If we come into contact with the anxious space invader, only to feel invaded and unsettled by their bolshy behaviour. Rather than seeing it for what it truly is, we will simply just escalate the feelings for the horse and give them no one to turn to. By the same token, if we are weak and allow the non anxious horse, the bloshy space invader to repeatedly invade our personal space. We are sending out the message that this is acceptable. Not only will this make it harder for us physically; it also makes it harder to gain the horses respect. In allowing it to continue we are not doing the horse any favours, as we are denying him the vital tuition of spatial awareness of others. This in turn could cause fights within his herd and further down the line, he may be heavily reprimanded by other trainers that do not have such a compassionate outlook.

All of this makes the horse that politely wishes to kiss, nuzzle and stand quietly and respectfully beside you, seem kind of perfect does it not?

This is because these kinds of interactions are based on friendship and mutual respect. There is an open invite extended to the ones that we feel comfortable with, due to the way in which we feel about them and they us. Neither invades the other's space or feels invaded upon the other party entering their own. It is simply acknowledged as the gift it is - acknowledgment of the other individual. This in mind, the way in which we also acknowledge our horse is of utmost importance. The gentle offering of a hand to sniff, or a gentle touch is acceptable to the horse before further physical contact is made. Such is the way of mutual respect and partnership. The fact of the matter is that when those two things happily exist and are maintained within a true partnership. We need not really pay our physical actions much mind, as our physical bodies will simply act out in the gentle, respectful way that our heart feels - The way in which we 'touch' our horse, quite literally being the extension of our heart and our respect that we hold for them as an individual.

Issues often arise when the horse or person invades the other parties' space, yet it does not feel invasive to that other party. This means there is an element of invasion that is not being recognised and kindly corrected. This will lead to an imbalance within the relationship, until this issue is rectified and the status quo of balance is restored.

How Do We Solve The Issue And Even Begin To Recognise It?

Each party – both horse and human must find the ability to go into their heart. Neither of you can feel the need to invade, or feel invaded by the other, when such interactions are heart felt and balance within the relationship reins. Heart interaction and connection is key - it creates acknowledgment.

The Horse Must Listen To You

Really? That would mean we have to have something important to say, or express by way of information that is beneficial to the horse, does it not? Should the information that we are offering to the horse not be that of mutual communication? Hearing and not just listening?

Cast your mind back if you will to the last time you had an uninteresting conversation. This maybe with someone that was so self absorbed that all they could talk about was themselves. Maybe they just fired out instructions that caused you to switch off. Or, it could be someone that used a dialogue of the type that you were not familiar. Maybe the person was quite frankly a plain bore that on some levels you found an insult to your level of intelligence, that they were unable to meet you on.

How did that make you feel?

Did they manage to hold your interest? I doubt it....

It is very much the same for the horse. He has no concern over the fact you are running late, or that your boss has put more work on your plate than you felt capable of coping with. Nor is he concerned with the fact you just hung your washing out and it is about to rain. So what - most likely he prefers you smelling or horse than washing powder anyway. Perfume just further confuses him. It masks the chemical signals that he needs to pick up from you that enables him to gauge your emotional state and physical health. Two of the important things the horse uses to assess you, mentally and physically to enable them to work out who you are.

What he cares about is mutual conversation and engagement - acknowledgment. When your horse is not listening to you, it is because of you. You are not gaining his focus and engaging with him in a way that is of benefit to him, or to the partnership in that moment in time. You are sending out the wrong information - information that he is unable to understand or act upon. All he knows is that what you are sending out at any given time feels comfortable and interesting, or negative and confusing. If this wrong information is attached to negative emotion, he will feel that from you. He will step back mentally and further close down to the information that is being sent his way. Whilst this is happening, something else is playing out too. You are not listening to your horse. This is the very same scenario that caused you to switch off from that last boring conversation that you had with that uninteresting person. The same one that caused you to wish they would be quiet, change their tune and connect with you - notice you, or go away. Engage with you in that moment, in something that was actually important to you - both of you and create the connection between the two of you that was sadly lacking in that moment in time.

When we allow ourselves to be weighed down by negative emotion, we dwell on it and it eats us alive. It quite literally eats us from the inside, right through to our outer layers. The inner munching away and deterioration will have a negative effect on our emotional state long term. The more we feed the emotion, the stronger it becomes. As our positive emotional state diminishes and our heart starts to close in anger, our body language will change and become negative, rather than being flowing, natural and of comfort to the horse. We will speed up, be more direct and yet less focused – confusing to him. This in turns sends out different and uncomfortable signals to the horse. Signals that are further confused, as we try and reinstate equilibrium within our emotional state. This often causes us to flit forwards and backwards, as the array of emotions and body language that we give off, further cause confusion for the horse.

You've lost him - there is nothing you have to say at that moment in time that he wants or needs to hear.

Should our horse in light of this have to listen to us all the time?

Hear him - not just the sound of your own voice and body language. You need to hear his too, to enable connection to be made. Only then will you be of interest and mutual benefit and partnership will be enabled. Only then will he be willing and opening to hearing what you have to say.

Focus on him, listen to him....he then in turn will want and desire to hear what you have to say.

You Need To Keep The Horse Moving

Why do we need to keep his feet moving?

To gain control of him through his movement?

To make him feel uncomfortable so that he wants to be with us?

Whilst it can be useful to keep a horse moving if he refuses to be caught for example. The idea of keeping his feet moving, to cause him to want to be with us when he feels uncomfortable or tires, is not really getting to the fundamental and underlying issue of why he does not want to be caught in the first place.

If we find the need to keep his feet moving, we have not actually found out the cause of the presenting issue. Rather, it just simply shows us a way of using what we know can work to correct the issue on a superficial level.

We should not need to control a horse, as the horse when relaxed, comfortable and trusting of his handler will not need to be 'controlled'.

I Am Training This Horse

Really?

There seems to be a general assumption within the equestrian world that we 'teach horses'. When in actual fact what we are teaching them is 'how we want them to do it', not necessarily the correct way for it to be done.

Let us take Dressage for an example: No end of pulled in heads with flash nosebands and over bend horses. By creating this false frame for the horse, we take away his innate ability to instead teach us. For him to show us how he moves, where his head is best comfortable and how he needs to hold himself to best carry his rider.

The sad truth is that most forms of tack are designed to control a horse in some way. Add to this the array of training aids that we see in our local tack shops and it is easy to see, just how much equipment people have come to rely on.

By stripping all of this commercial cost away, (our financial cost and the physical and emotional cost to the horse) we are able to go back to the raw horse, the one that can instead teach us. We can enable him to *teach us* how he understands it needs to be done. Show us how he best feels comfortable and how his body moves, so that we can learn how best to move with him.

The moment we decide we are 'training this horse'. We close our mind to the mutual teaching that is able to be experienced in each of our horse encounters. Listen to him; let him teach you for a change. Put down the reins for a while and let him be your teacher for a while. You will be surprised at just how much he has to offer you through his own knowledge.

NEGATIVE REINFORCEMENT

Negative reinforcement is the training often used by some of the best known Natural Horsemanship trainers. This sadly is the very reason that I choose to steer clear of both them and their methods.

The act of negative reinforcement is to apply pressure to a horse in order to give instruction for a desired outcome. This pressure may come in the form of mental or physical pressure, but due to physical pressure mental pressure will usually be present too.

In the case of negative reinforcement the pressure is applied as instruction for a certain outcome. Here I will give a few examples:

Applying pressure to the chest to ask the horse to back up

Applying pressure to a long lead rope in the form of movement, to cause the horse to back up

Tightening pressure and pushing backwards holding a lead rope to make the horse move back

Squeezing the chestnuts, knee or other area of the leg to make them lift it

Taking up pressure on and pulling back on the reins, to cause the horse to stop or back up

'Sending a horse 'away' as in 'join up'

Backing a horse up using pressure when refusing to enter a horse trailer or lorry

Negative reinforcement trainers apply the pressure and then release it, once the horse gives the desired response. Problems can arise when a horse is stressed and suffering from anxiety. This will make it harder for the horse to concentrate. They will feel more concerned about their surroundings and what else is going on - due to this their full concentration will not be on you. When it is not on you, chances are extra pressure has to be applied to them to bring it more into their awareness. Over and above the other things in their environment which may also be causing them concern.

I have seen cases of enormous and cruel pressure being applied. Some examples of this were at some live horse demonstrations. In one case a horse was being loaded into a trailer in a Dually halter. This is like a head collar but has the addition of two pieces of rope that go over the nose along with the nose band. Out through the rings at the side and then the lead rope is attached to one end of the rope by way of another ring.

The horse was refusing to walk into the trailer. The 'Why?', sadly was not questioned; the handler just wanted him in there. Each time he refused, pressure was applied to the horse's face by way of the Dually being pulled down on his nose and on the sensitive bones situated there, causing him to back up. Sadly due to poor design, the two rings at each end of the rope are not long enough to couple together to apply even pressure. So this caused the rope part of the noseband to slip sideways and also apply pressure underneath one of the horse's eyes. The two thin pieces of rope are also rounded, so the actual pressure area is very limited and not spread out. This also increases the discomfort of the pressure.

The lead rope was yanked several times causing physical discomfort to the horse and was only stopped once he had backed up. Once he had backed up, he was asked again to walk forwards. When he refused this whole story and uncomfortable process was repeated until he gave up, walked forward and entered. He had been bullied into loading with no concern over his refusal to load, no time to explore and get used to the trailer and with a handler he did not know. To me this is the pittance of negative horsemanship and a failing of the horse.

Another example of negative reinforcement that is in no way productive and is exceptionally unfair to the horse is a well known, 'backing up game'. A long rope is clipped onto the horse's rope halter or head collar. The handler stands facing the horse and 'wiggles' the rope, as a way of teaching the horse to back up away from the pressure. Once the horse takes a step back the 'wiggle' pressure is stopped. Problem being that the rope is in momentum and if the horse by now has backed up several steps. The reward 'the stopping of the pressure' is not instant, even though the horse has offered correct behaviour, as the rope takes a moment to stop moving. Add to this the metal clip that is banging him under the chin and it is a scene that is not a kind one.

Many years ago I attended a Chiropractic course for horse owners. We worked with eight horses on the course. Five of those eight horses all had varying degrees of Lumber Facet Syndrome. (Interestingly all of these horses were jumpers). This basically means that physically it was uncomfortable for them to go backwards.

Now let us return to the backing up game. Pressure is applied, the horse wants to move backwards to enable the pressure to stop, but if he does it may hurt, in fact it may hurt more than the pressure being applied by the trainer. So what does he do? He does nothing - he is stuck between a rock and a hard place. Whatever he does will be uncomfortable, so he chooses to go with the least discomfort by way of his response - he does not back up. The trainer then thinks he is refusing to obey (In fact they may even be getting frustrated with this 'naughty' horse by now.) and a more forceful 'wiggle' is applied. In fact it keeps being applied and escalated, until such a time that the level of discomfort and pressure overrides the discomfort the horse, may know he will feel physically moving backwards. So he moves backwards - trainer relaxes, he has his desired response, but at what cost to the horse?

At this point I also think it worth mentioning that this medical issue is largely, but not solely, responsible for horses reversing out of rear loading trailers too quickly. Whilst the horse may unload backwards too fast due to concern over the trailer and wanting to get off of it, or concern over what is behind them and wanting to unload quickly so that they can see. Often, the cause is pain that the horse knows he will feel going backwards, so wishes to unload as quickly as possible and get it over and done with.

Let us now take a look at negative reinforcement in riding. At the beginning of this chapter I have already given one example of negative reinforcement being used in the case of backing the horse up, or stopping him. Most training that is carried out in a traditional manner is based on negative reinforcement. Pressure is applied creating discomfort so the horse looks to move away from the pressure. Pressure is applied by legs, maybe a whip, movement in the seat in the form of rocking and through the bit on the sensitive nerves and soft tissues of the mouth and maybe also the poll. In the case of a bitless bridle, this may be in the form of poll pressure and pressure on the sensitive nasal bones that sit just underneath the skin.

During a conversation with a horse trainer he offered some insightful advice. One day a man turn up for a riding lesson with him, complete with all his tack. The trainer asked him if he needed the saddle and reins. The rider replied that he did, so the trainer told him he could not have them until he had no use for them. He then proceeded to teach him to ride by way of his seat and natural balance. Once the man was able to maintain his own balance and not use the stirrups, reins and horse's mouth to balance, he was allowed his tack back. If only more trainers and instructors worked this way!

Let us look at rein contact; some horses will feel secure with rein contact when gentle hands are holding the other end and instructing kindly and not applying 'pressure'. The problem comes when the reins are used to steer the horse through his mouth and face, applying painful pressure. This may well be escalated by the rider's need, to use the reins for balancing himself in the saddle. When this has become a habit and the rider is either unaware of his rein contact, or unable to do anything about it. There is no release for the horse and no reward for what is offered by him, for his correct response. In my humble opinion - until such a time that we are able to ride from our seat and not rely on rein pressure, we have no business using rein contact. This will only cause the horse to suffer discomfort in his mouth and maybe in his face as well.

I have seen horses whose only form of training and preparation for being ridden is to hop on, take up rein contact and 'off we go'. Is this fair? What exactly is this telling the horse? Further more what it is meant to teach him other than humans do not listen and are selectively ignorant to a horse's needs?

All riding training starts on the ground. Can you stop your horse without applying pressure to him through his mouth and head? Can you ask him to walk, trot and canter and back up without applying pressure on the ground? If your answer is 'no' then your preparation for riding is not in place. If you are unable to do this on the ground through positive cues, then it stands to reason that you will only achieve this in the saddle through force being applied in the form of pressure and discomfort. All ridden education starts from and on the ground.

What is force?

Here is a list of words that are associated with force:

Power, strength, exertion, coercion, duress, enforcement, harassment, intimidation and threats.

Not nice are they?

However everyday throughout the world horses are being treated and trained with force.

Your horse does not understand when you hit him, or when you wave a coloured stick around, or a whip. He only knows he needs to move away from these things. He does not understand shouting, other than in the context of the tone and unsettling feeling that the tone brings to him. He does not understand conflicting signals, requests and cues from you, anymore than he understands punishment inflicted on him. He was quite simply offering his response to the behaviour that you offered him. Abuse breeds abuse; if we are unkind to our horse and we abuse his sensitive nature, we risk either him shutting down emotionally and mentally, or we risk him retaliating in a violent manner. Neither is of benefit to us or our horse and neither of these are acceptable in the world of horsemanship and within our relationships with our horses. Instead, let us seek to find peace, respect and understanding within our relationships. Thus enabling quiet calm and focus to rein, that we may understand each other and work together in harmony.

Let us ride him gently, without his having to experience the use of force on the reins and pain in his mouth and around his face. Let him view us as a friend not a foe; creating an environment that he seeks to share with us because he chooses to.

When we choose to use force, not only can it bring psychological devastation, a break down of trust, negative biological functions and physical pain. It ruins any chance we have of the horse wanting to be in our company. It creates an environment where his work and his experiences of being with you are negative and unwanted - sometimes even dreaded.

Cast your mind back to meeting someone you found demanding, that made you feel uncomfortable and that was loud and rude.

How did it make you feel?

Is this how you want your horse to feel?

So how can we change 'force' to 'touch'?

When we use 'touch' instead of 'force', we are then using gentleness and instruction, thereby neutralising the need for force. It enables the horse to remain calm and focused. His senses and biological functions remain lowered and do not override him in a manner he is unable to cope with. He is able to think and look for all the possible explanations and answers and search within them, to find the one that you are asking for. The touching of his physical body causes him to become thoughtful rather than fretful. He welcomes the touch to aid him in the search for answers in the hope of acknowledgment reward.

I feel before ending this chapter I need to explain something. Negative reinforcement is not all bad; in fact, at times it is needed and so becomes positive. It is the way in which it is applied that creates the feelings of negative or positive for the horse. The harm and confusion is created when only negative reinforcement is offered and applied. It can in fact be argued that in certain situations, negative reinforcement becomes positive reinforcement. This will be largely down to agenda, energy and focus of the trainer and their application of instruction. We also have neutral offerings in our tool kit that we can offer the horse. This too is something that I will be explaining in depth in my next book, *Horsemanship - The Revelations.*

This now leads us to the opposite end of the

scale - the kinder more considerate and respectful approach of positive reinforcement in training.

POSITIVE REINFORCEMENT

Positive reinforcement works on the basis of ignoring the unwanted behaviour and rewarding for the correct behaviour offered by the horse. The reward may come in the form of a food reward, such as used in clicker training, or it may come in the form of a physical touch that is pleasant for the horse, such as a rub or a scratch in a favourite area.

Instruction may be given to the horse in the form of a gentle touch or a key word, that the horse has previously learnt and therefore is familiar with and understands it meaning. This is then followed up with the reward in the form of the rub or scratch. Due to this being a pleasant experience for the horse, he will choose to seek the behaviour that you are asking for, rather than choosing to ignore you or feeling under any duress to comply. Quite simply, he has a choice whether to engage and follow your request. The fact that there is something in it for him; something he likes, he seeks to follow your instruction.

This allows for a calm, focused and positive outlook towards training our horses. It enables their heart rate to stay low, breathing to remain normal and not become too fast, laboured or held in. When we also remain calm, breathe and relax, we are able to give our horse our full focus and observe and recognise his every offering and behaviour. Without being distracted by what else is going on.

Before I carry on, I would like to clear up a myth that tends to exist over food rewards. Many people choose not to feed their horse rewards or engage in clicker training. As they feel that this encourages 'mugging' and biting. My advice is this: If your horse is mugging you and biting you, then you are not carrying out the training the correct way. When carried out correctly, a horse will not mug you for the food reward or bite you out of frustration, when it does not come quickly enough. If you are training him correctly, he will know that the reward in the form of the food will only come when he is working with you through choice and not, when he is focused on food and not you. Simply put, if you reward him by letting him have the food when he is biting or mugging, or immediately after the event, you have just rewarded him for doing so. You have unwittingly trained him to mug and bite you. Sadly, this is an all too familiar story that has caused many people to dismiss the positives of clicker training.

Personally when I begin positive reinforcement training with a horse, rather than use a food reward and clicker. I prefer to use voice for cue and request, and touch for reward. The reason for this is that when we are holding a clicker and having to dip into a pocket or pouch each time. Not only is it distracting for us, it can also be time consuming. It can cause us to miss vital cues and be late with rewards, which can at times cause confusion for the horse. Our voice and hands are right on cue when used correctly and with good timing. The only times I tend to revert to a clicker and a food reward. Is when a horse may feel anxious or is easily distracted. An example of these instances is introducing a horse to traffic, his first walk out on the road and loading a concerned horse into a trailer.

Please be aware that if you choose to go down the clicker and food reward path. You must make sure that reward is available at the time it is needed. By causing a delay due to having to rummage around in your pocket for the food, you will have missed the cue your horse needs to tell him his behaviour and response was correct. This may then cause him to continue to search for what you are asking for, when he has already offered it to you, or cause him to become frustrated.

I will now give some examples of how I use positive reinforcement to train my horses.

Backing Up

To teach my horses to back up, I put a gentle hand on their chest and use the word 'back'. If they do not do it immediately, I pause for a few seconds, increase the 'touch' slightly *but without force* and repeat the word 'back'. The *moment* my horse gives me any form of positive response to my request. I use the words 'good boy' and give him a good scratch. We then repeat the process again in the same consistent manner, to reinforce the cues and responses. This causes him to search for the behaviour being asked for, in order to create the reward he seeks. I am not applying 'pressure' until he chooses to 'comply'. It is within the method and intention that the negative order is bypassed and positive request is created.

It will only take two or three attempts for my horses to fully have the understanding, that this is the desired response to my request. The first time they will understand it, the second and third times are purely to reinforce that 'yes', this is correct, to enable them to be sure in their own minds. From here they learn that a hand near their chest, but not touching them means a request to 'back up'. Once this has been established, no hand is needed and the word 'back', is enough on its own. Throughout this form of training I will reward with a good scratch on cue and use the words 'good boy' as soon as the positive response is offered, however subtle that may be.

My horses have learnt by now that touch, plus a word equals a request for which they will be rewarded for following. This causes them to seek the answer, by way of their response to my request, willingly with no use for force.

Picking Up A Hoof

In order to teach a horse to pick up a hoof and leg, I will first touch the leg at the same time as I use the word 'leg'. The horse then searches for what it is I am asking him. The moment he shifts his weight and lightens it on that leg, I will say 'good boy' and reward him. We then repeat the process until he is lifting his leg. From here he will learn that touching his leg, or using the word 'leg' is the request and instruction to lift it. Each time this is offered by him on request, he is rewarded.

This now leads me on to positive reinforcement for food muggers. One of my Arabians was a dreadful food mugger. I was not using food rewards with him, but if he thought I had food on me he would become obsessed with getting it. Now and again he would become frustrated and bite me. He would try and rummage in my pockets and became a general pest when he thought food was available to him.

Rather than punish him for this behaviour; punish him for demanding food. I chose to teach him to ask for it nicely, especially as he is also handled by a young child. This was also important in case I wanted to later go down the route of clicker training with him. I did not want to install in him the thought that food must be ignored, but rather that it comes as a reward during training. To do this if he searched me for food I would ask him to stand quietly. As soon as he did I would reward him and then ask him to lift his leg. As soon as he did I offered him a food reward. He now understands that in order to get the food that I have with me, he must stand quietly and lift his leg (his horse version of 'please') and he knows it will then quietly be forth coming.

When horses mug us for food, not only if it annoying and stressful for us. It is also confusing and stressful for them. If they know you have food on you and you are pushing them away and not giving it to them, it becomes out of bounds, yet is still there and this can lead to frustration. In some cases this can escalate behaviour in the form of biting and barging. This in mind, teaching horses how to ask for food and how to respond when food is available is very important, not just for general manners, but also from a safety point of view.

When I am carrying food buckets across a field at dinner time, my horses know to walk along side me to where the buckets will be put down. Should they get a little excited that dinner is coming then the simple word 'ah' works well, as a cue for 'behave yourself it is coming in due course!' They then walk with me nicely. My young horse is sometimes so excited that he will suddenly run off, do a circle and a buck or two and then go back to a quiet walk and join me again. We have no barging, swapping of food buckets or mugging, as the buckets are put on the ground. My horses are calm as they know the process and that dinner is arriving very soon in a non stressful way.

Consistency counts for everything; horses learn through consistency and repeat. Always be black and white in your instruction, with no grey areas that may be hard for your horse to understand. Make sure that *you* are sure of what you are asking them to do, to enable your instruction and cue to be clear for them. If you are not sure of what you are asking them, how can you expect them to know what you are asking? Reward is of the utmost importance, not only does it cause the horse to seek the behaviour and response that you are seeking, but it also enables him to know that he has found exactly what you are looking for. He then knows that he need no longer keep seeking a correct response to offer you.

He needs to know he has got it right.

I add to this further by introducing the word 'no', but not in the negative sense, or as a way of telling a horse off. But rather, as an instruction to him that the behaviour he is offering is not what

I am looking for. The positive side to this is that, it enables him to stop looking in the wrong direction and to change in his thought and search in another direction, the correct one. The word 'no' in my herd is always used positively, we do not seek to punish or use force.

Being aware of our speech and how much we use it, is also very important. When we are with our horses and keep chattering to them, or another person and we are placing some of our focus on our horse. We are causing him to have to keyword search in amongst the words of random conversation. Most of what we are saying will sound double dutch to him, but he will intently be listening for what he does understand. When we use keywords within conversation and it does not relate to what is going on. It can cause confusion for our horses. In these circumstances being as your focus is partly on him, he is looking to you for instruction, as he thinks that you are talking to him. This may be unavoidable at time if we have other people with us that we need to speak to, when in the company of our horse. Please do try and make it clear to your horse as to whether he is your focus at that time, or the person is your focus within the conversation, this will help him.

Positive Reinforcement And Reward In Play

When I am training horses, my favoured method is to do this at liberty. Meaning the horse is not tied, not wearing a head collar and is free to move away from me. This is important as even the moving away and disengagement of the horses focus from us; is huge information in itself for the trainer.

I shall use the example of how I have used positive reinforcement to teach horses what I call 'The Bending Game'.

I begin by first asking the horse to 'walk on' and 'whoa' along side me. To do this I use the words, 'walk on' and 'whoa' and reward each time they offer the correct response. This is the basis for all of my training, including ridden work. Next I stand to the right of him by his ribs, with my left hand on his wither. I then tap my right hip with my right hand, whilst saying the word 'bend'. This causes him to turn his head towards my hip in order to explore the sound and movement he has become aware of, in that area. As soon as he does this, I use the words 'good boy', as the cue that this is the desired response and scratch him on his wither as his reward.

I then step around to the other side of him and repeat the process.

He has now learnt that the word 'bend' is his cue, to bend his head round to my hip, for which he will be rewarded. Once the horse has understood that this is the desired response I am seeking from him. I will ask him to 'walk on' along side me. I then ask him to 'Whoa', place my hand on his wither, use the word 'bend' and when he bends round, I use the words 'good boy' and scratch his wither again.

Once this sequence has been fully established, we move it up a gear. When I ask the horse to 'walk on' he knows it is now his cue to move forwards. He is seeking his reward, so when I run he keeps pace with me, when I stop, he stops along side me. I place my hand on his wither. He then bends which I then follow through with his scratch. Usually I will only have to repeat this sequence with a horse two or three times for him to fully understand and get it consistently correct. Once this has happened, the horse will run with me, stop with me and then bend on cue when a hand is place on his wither, no words are then needed.

This is just one of many games that we can teach our horses at liberty and in play, through positive reinforcement. The beauty of it is that there is no punishment for the horse. He does not have to worry about getting it wrong and he is seeking to get it right. He is looking to engage with you - he is seeking to be in your company, due to the pleasant feelings and experience it brings for him.

The reason I like the bending game along with

bowing, is that they are two fold. Not only are they fun for the horse, but they are also beneficial for them physically. These games and exercises allow for the stretching of muscles and the spine, in a way that the horse has control over without injury or discomfort. They are also a good visual barometer for how supple your horse is. If you are seeing that he is a little stiff, you will find that the more you invite him to engage in these games with you, the more beneficial it will be to him. His muscles begin to release and the bending becomes much easier for him.

These games are hard to use for the intention of aiding physical flexibility when taught with the use of negative reinforcement. When used with negative reinforcement there will be a degree of concern for the horse that will not allow his body and mind to relax in the same way. This will stop him from relaxing his muscles and enabling him to feel the full benefit of these wonderful exercises that disguised in the form of fun games. Never forget to feel the fun in them. When the fun is lacking - seek to explore a better way.

What is missing within your game that has caused it to cease being fun?

Why is your horse not engaging with you in it?

Is he feeling ill?

Sore?

Are you in a negative state of mind, but putting on a smiley face for his benefit?

Are your cues correct?

Have you over done it and repeated this game a little too often?

Maybe today is just not a day he feels like playing. Maybe the game is too upbeat for his relaxed mood? Or too boring for his excited mood today and he wishes to explore more in other directions. Pick your moments and set both you and your horse up to succeed.

THE LEADING ROLE

There is a commonly held belief in the equestrian world that the owner of a horse, should take on the role and status of leader within the relationship and interaction between horse and owner and or rider.

But how true is this exactly?

Is our rightful role as leader?

Do we need to remain as leader?

How do we achieve the status of leader?

In a wild herd of horses and to a large degree in domesticated herds, there will be an obvious leader. The role of the leader is to aid in the smooth running of the herd, deal with any rebels, keep the herd safe and well organised and in some cases help to set boundaries for the younger members. In the form of a mixed herd the leader will often be a mare, though this is not always set in stone.

How And Why Leadership Changes

Whilst on observation it may appear that there is only one leader, the truth of the matter is that this can change. Each individual in the herd will have their own unique strengths and weaknesses. The role of the lead member of the herd may actually change, dependent on what is actually playing out in the herd at any given time. Let us take for instance the example of three members of the herd all being ridden out together, including the lead mare. It maybe the case that whilst the primary leader, in this case the lead mare feels secure and confident in her role in the field, which involves the day to day care and organisation of her herd. She may not be so confident once away from part of it and in a different environment. She may be traffic shy, or only concerned over larger vehicles. She may be a novice riding horse that has little experience, or she may not have ventured out of her field much prior to recently being introduced to her ridden work.

For one or more of these reasons whilst out being ridden, she may choose to stand back and allow another more confident horse to take the leading role. If she does, then this is a good indicator of a leader that fully understands her role as protector of the herd and her own limitations. She is aware that she is unable to do the best for her herd in this environment, so in order to help them and keep them safe. She allows another to take her place that is further able to help the herd at that moment in time. A mare that would refuse to stand down in these circumstances would likely be one that is more concerned over her status, than the true safety of her herd.

Other circumstances where we may see a change in the leader of the herd and how it may shift to another member. Is if the lead mare is not fully comfortable with strangers, or people in general. This may be seen as a new person entering into the field with the herd. The lead mare may choose to stand back and allow another herd member to take on the lead role as herd protector. She will allow the other horse to step forward to explore this new person, making sure that they are acceptable and safe to let in. As the role of herd leader has shifted, the other herd members will have become aware and willing to accept the decision as being safe for them as a whole.

Let us remember that in order for another herd member to take on the role as leader in certain circumstances, he can only do it with permission of the other herd members. Without such permission being granted, he may be challenged by other members that feel they are more capable.

This taken into consideration, it is important to view ourselves as the leader only 'when needed'. It may be that we are a novice rider and whilst out riding we need to take a back seat and allow our confident horse to take the leading role and listen to him when he suspects danger, instead of overriding his judgement. Or it may be that you are new to jumping and are onboard a confident show jumper and you just sit back and allow him to do what he does best, without hindering or questioning him.

Each horse with his own unique personality traits, will have something to bring to the table for us to experience. If we choose to take on the role as leader on a permanent basis, then we may well be denying ourselves valuable experiences and lessons from our horses. As well as denying them their rightful role at that time.

Through training with positive reinforcement rather than negative reinforcement, we enable the horse to work 'with us' not 'for us', or under our 'command'. When we enable this, the role of leader in the games and training between horse and human will shift. Not only now is our horse learning in a healthy and productive environment, but he is also teaching us.

Should your horse choose to take a dislike to someone, you would be wise to take note. Keep in mind though, the role that person is in, in relation to the horse. If he is a Farrier and your horse is sore or has had a previous bad experience, or he is a chiropractor and your horse has some skeletal issues, his wariness of the person may be down to that. But if his negative response is out of the blue with no obvious reason, it may well be the case that he is picking up on something about this person, through their energy and body language. Some horses are so intuitive and aware in this way that you can literally pick your friends by them.

Leadership In Therapy

Up until a few years ago I was working with Equine Facilitated Therapy. This is a therapy in which the horse takes on the leading role as therapist. They mirror the behaviour of their clients, with the human therapist as their 'co-helper'. My best horse for working with people was my chestnut Arabian, Alfi. His ability to recognise someone and what was underlying, the moment that they walked into his field, was second to none.

One day I had a call from a lady that wanted to book herself in for a session with us. When I put the phone down I must admit, I was already dreading it. The lady I had spoken to was very forth right, out spoken and made me feel uncomfortable. This was exactly the type of person that Alfi did not like and I had images of him taking an instant dislike to her and may be even biting her.

The day came, the lady arrived and we started off

by having a chat over coffee, as she had just driven for several hours. She told me that she felt she didn't need therapy. The reason she had booked me was because her mother thought she needed to. Once we had finished our drinks, we made our way out to the field where my horses were grazing. I waited at the gate and asked the lady if she was happy to go into the field alone. She was, so I just stood and waited and observed.

Alfi lifted his head, looked at her for a few seconds and then made his way to her. He came to a standstill about six feet in front of her, staring her square in the eye with the utmost respect. It was in this moment that I realised that I had misjudged this lady and badly. There was something there that Alfi was recognising in her, something that was honest and worthy of his respect. Baring in mind that in order to gain this horse's respect you have to earn it. He is not the sort of personality that will give unwillingly of falsely. He is too honest and knowing for that.

Needless to say the rest of the session went well and Alfi stood up to his reputation of being the excellent Therapist. At the end of the day I was so touched by the interaction between the two of them, that I made the decision to tell her what I had thought and why. I also explained to the lady that it was through her interaction with Alfi and what he had shown me through his behaviour towards her, that I realised I was wrong. I then apologised to her. Her response was to smile and say 'thank you'. It was not mentioned again, it did not need to be. Both of us were safe in the knowledge that Alfi had carried out his role perfectly, not just for the lady, but in teaching me a lesson about judgment also.

Leadership In Ridden Work

When we are riding our horse, a balance will need to be found between who is leading who. Ideally our horse will be a quiet confident type that is able to go up a gear at the flick of a switch if requested. He will stop on cue and listen tentatively to our requests and offer the correct responses. Of course this is not always the idyllic case and indeed should not always be the case.

Due to the lack of training and schooling in some horses and novice riders and the relationships that are formed between the two, problems at some point are sure to arise. We must not judge our horse on our own ability, but rather on his own.

What is he capable of?

What does he understand?

What are his strengths?

What are his weaknesses?

What does he detest?

What does he enjoy?

Only too often, the horse will get the blame when things go wrong. When all they have in fact been doing is following the lead and instruction of their rider. A typical example of this, is a horse following his rider's cues up to a jump and then running out at the last minute. Unless the horse has been distracted by something in his environment or pain, chances are he has followed his riders lead all too perfectly and arrived at the jump ill paced, or on a poor angle for take on and a clear jump.

A knowledgeable horse that is respected and is listening to his rider, will have the confidence to ignore wrong request. He may make his own corrections without fear of punishment, or the rider trying to over ride him. Leading to a perfect jump that is well balanced, where the rider sits correctly and allows him to do what and how he does it best.

In the case of the novice riding horse the roles may change. The horse may be unsure and come up against things that he is unfamiliar with. In this instance he will need a confident rider who does not show fear, is able to relax and feed him confidence through their calm demeanour. As an example of this, I will use a scary carrier bag in a hedge. As the horse approaches it and sees, it he may do one of several things. He may slow, shy, spin and turn, or step side ways and bend his body to walk past it in a way that it still remains in view, or he may try to run.

A rider that is able and willing to take on the role of leadership and help install confidence and education into a horse like this, will have spotted the carrier bag as soon as the horse has, if not before. She will breathe out and touch her horse to reassure him and let him know she is there and aware, helping him understand that he is not alone. Her body will remain relaxed and without tension, so as not to give the horse a wrong cue that she is ready to flee. She will then observe the horse's reactions and this is where it gets interesting. As there are two techniques that can be used in this situation that are not commonly used and yet work so well.

We need to remember that the moment the horse has noticed the carrier bag; his focus has shifted from us to the bag. He is now in the mental state of 'Focusing on scary object, instead of what can help keep me safe'. So how can we change this? We have two options. Both options do and need to include the changing of the focus. The way in which we do this is to ask the horse to do something. A common way of doing this is that if the horse is trying to move away from the object, the rider will put a leg on them to stop them moving away further, or to keep them still. When this happens all we are doing is helping the horse refocus on his fear - not helpful. So let us try two other options.

Option 1

We ask the horse to do something that is easy for him to do and known to him; something that he has done many times before. His focus shifts back to us as he listens. Once we have regained his focus, we can then ask him to move forwards again. This request may come in the form of backing up, turning his head, a leg yield, basically anything that enables us to gain his focus. As when his focus is on us, it is not on the carrier bag.

Option 2

If the horse has moved away from the bag on approaching it, rather than putting a leg on him to keep him still so he can look at it, instead use your leg to move him *away* from it. He will wonder why you are moving him away and when done calmly as you are asking him to do what he would like to do, he is likely to follow your instruction. Again bringing his focus back to you where you can then ask for your next cue.

There is also a school of thought that says we should encourage the horse to stand and look at the scary object, in order that he can see that it is not going to leap out and bite him. Though on first consideration of this it may make sense, we must consider the fact that by doing this we are also creating a situation where the object actually deserves focus. Is it not actually better not to create a fuss and accept it as just part of the riding environment, to enable our horse to feel that way too? Does a carry bag really deserve our focus? If he looks, show him it is not worth his focus and that his focus and security lies in you, in this instance his leader, allow him to follow your lead.

Although I have only covered two examples of how the leadership role can change during ridden work. I am sure you are able to think of many more. The more out of the box thinking and forward thinking we can be, exploring things from all angles. The more help and use we will be to not only our horse, but also our relationship with him.

Simply put - we do not get it right all of the time. Sometimes we just need to accept that he knows best. Put down the reins and let him show us how. If we choose never to do that, then not only do we deny our horse his sometimes earnt and rightful role as our leader and teacher. But we also deny ourselves those insightful experiences from which we can learn from him.

STEREOTYPICAL BEHAVIOUR AND VICES

Many of you will be familiar with vices; the behaviours that some horses can display which include:

Weaving - Shifting weight from one front leg to the other, whilst weaving the head from side to side.

Wind-sucking - Holding onto a fence, wooden post or the top of a stable door -whilst gulping in air.

Box walking - Walking up and down a fence line or stable and back again - repeatedly.

Cribbing - Biting fencing and the top of stable doors and wooden posts.

In most instances it will be some kind of trauma, stress or boredom that has resulted in these behaviours, these may include:

Early weaning

Lack of food

Pain

Living alone

When a companion is removed from their company

Stabling and other forms of forced confinement

Being bullied

Harsh owner or care giver

Novice and confusing owner or care giver

The physical act of these behaviours aids in the release of endorphins. These are the body's natural pain relief chemicals and feel good chemicals. In the case of wind-sucking stomach ulcers may be involved, due to anxiety or poor feeding that enables the body to reach a acidity PH that is harmful to the horse. In some cases the wind-sucking will help to relieve the stomach discomfort, whilst the ulcers may have occurred due to stress in the first place.

If you have observed a horse with these types of

behaviours, one thing that is always apparent is the glazed look in their eye, the vacant 'no-one is home' look. This is actually quite close to the truth, as during these times no body is at home, in as much as the horses has allowed himself to go inward and removed himself from his everyday consciousness as a way of coping. In some instances even waving a hand in front of their face, touching them or calling them will bring no response at all.

Ulcers can be very serious in horses and lead to a lot of pain. In some instances they can be responsible for the onset of certain types of colic. If the horse is stressed, not being fed suitable food, or has a lack of food, ulcers are likely to be there to some degree.

Studies have shown that horses on racing yards tend to have high levels of ulcers - as many as 70-90% of horses on any one yard.

Ulcers should never be taken lightly, if you suspect that your horse has them, veterinary advice should be taken immediately.

Symptoms of ulcers may include:

Looking tight and tucked up in their abdominal area, refusal or lack of interest in hard food that they are usually happy to eat, wind-sucking, unhappy to have their girth tightened when there has previously been no issue with this. They may come across as quiet, grumpy, or sensitive to touch. They may display tightness in their back end, including the hind legs.

A good indicator of the health of the horse is their urine. Not only the PH of it to show whether it is too acid or too alkaline, but also to see if it shows any signs of blood, if it is thick, cloudy or abnormally smelly. If any obvious changes to urine are seen, or if the above signs are present, then this is a good indicator that there is an issue that may well need looking into. This may include tests for organ function, for toxins and the lymphatic system.

The liver and kidneys also play a vital role in helping the keep the digestive system healthy. The kidneys help to clean and filter the fluids of the body and release any toxins through the urine. The liver also helps rid the body of toxins through droppings. The liver plays a vital role in creating liver bile that the horse needs for digesting his food properly. When the liver is compromised, not only will the horse have issues with trying to rid his body of toxins, but he will also likely have a compromised digestive system. In major acute or chronic cases this may cause the skin of the horse to smell unhealthy, as well as the droppings.

That said, any of these vices and the stresses involved can lead to ulcers, it is just that wind-sucking is the one most indicative to them.

Once a vice has become engrained due to a stressful time, or event that later passes. It is possible that the vice then becomes habitual. By this I mean that the reason for the original onset of the vice is no longer present, but that the action and 'pull' to still display the behaviour is still there. By now the horse will also be aware and will have associated the physical action of the vice, with the releasing of the endorphins. This may further cause him to still engage in the behaviour, due to the good feelings that he has learnt it brings to him.

Another thing we need to consider once stress and anxiety is no longer present. Is if we are in fact rewarding the horse for continuing these behaviours. In order to explain what I mean by rewarding for these behaviours, I will relay to you the story of one of my now sadly passed mares, affectionately named 'Demolition Polly'. On account of her ability to smash things in her pathway, fencing, field shelters, the works.

I was asked to have Polly when she was around eighteen years old. She was a grey Arab X Welsh mare and very highly strung. In recent years she had been through three homes due to her behaviour, as people thought they could 'fix' her. One such home decided the best way to try and fix her was through spraying her with a hosepipe when she weaved. Needless to say this most certainly did not stop the behaviour and likely just escalated the stress and the physical presentation of her vice.

She also had a paralysed lower lip, due to the damage inflicted on the nerve through use of a curb chain in a previous home. I think you get the picture...

At the time Polly belonged to a good friend of mine. She lived out in a herd of six horses on around thirty acres of land with forest for shelter. This would be many horses' dream environment, but not for Polly. She wanted to be leader of the herd, but with youngsters that were better mentally balanced than her and younger than her eighteen years. She found herself repeatedly being challenged over her status. Not only this, but her neurotic threatening, screaming, bucking behaviour had little effect, as the other horses just did not take it seriously. Not only this, but she had also developed alopecia due to stress and had lost hair on her face and running down her front legs.

Due to this Polly found herself in a state of constant stress and her displays of weaving had continued. Due to knowing it was being caused by stress, her owner at the time did what she could to relieve it. Polly would be fed first, removed from the field first and receive the most attention. Due to her being an intelligent mare, she had also learnt that her weaving got her what she wanted, not only did it help her relieve stress, but she got her dinner first also.

This rewarded behaviour became apparent when Polly arrived home with me. As her owner and I both suspected, she got one fine with my existing mare. There was little issue between them, as Kayleigh made no attempt to challenge Polly. Within three weeks Polly's hair also started to grow back as her stress levels started to decline. Polly used to watch me as I walked towards the feed shed, all would be quiet until I appeared again with food bowls in my hand. The moment Polly saw the bowls she would be stood at the fence and the weaving would start.

One day my phone rang and I quickly turned and ran to get it. I answered it and turned round and looked in Polly's direction. She was no longer weaving and instead, had her head up watching me with her ears pricked. Whilst I continued my conversation she turned and walked away. This gave me a clue to her cause of behaviour. It showed me how both my self and her previous owner had been trained by Polly, due to feeling sorry for her. Although admittedly in earlier times Polly's weaving had been due to stress. She had also learnt that it brought her what she wanted, that was the cause of her weaving now.

From then on, each time I made Polly's dinner, I would leave it outside the feed shed and walk away out of sight. Once she had stopped weaving and walked away, I would then go and give her the bucket, so as not to reward her for her weaving. This worked well and it did not take long for the weaving to stop. I only ever saw it twice after that, both times due to neighbours letting off fireworks.

Once Polly realised the weaving was of no use, she did have one more final attempt at trying to train and control me over her dinner situation. When she knew her dinner was coming, she would reverse into the field shelter kicking the walls whilst screaming. She would then walk forward a few steps and poke her nose out, so that she could see me and to see if she was getting any reaction. She wasn't and again after a time once she was satisfied that this method would not work either, the behaviour stopped.

I feel it is important to point out that during this time Polly was not stressed, just annoyed and that her neurotic behaviour in many cases was tantrum related, not stress. Had Polly been stressed and had that been the cause of her weaving at this time, then I would have handled things differently. As the act of walking away and leaving her dinner and not giving it to her, would have caused her further stress. In such situations it is important that we fully understand the situation that is occurring, before we decide on a course of action that is in the best interests of our horse.

There are various anti-vice products for sale on line and in tack shops.

These will include:

A fowl tasting gel that you spread along fencing and the top of stable doors, in order to stop your horse from cribbing or wind-sucking. As well as, collars with a nutcracker action on the throat when the horse wind-sucks - both equally as horrid as each other.

My advice to you is this:

Do not use either of these products, or any others. The act of stopping a vice in this way is of no benefit to your horse and will only cause them further stress, or cause them to search for and maybe adopt another type of vice. By preventing the physical action of a vice, what you are doing is stopping the horse from being able to release endorphins. You are then stopping him from being able to calm himself and bring his stress levels down to a level that he can hopefully manage.

Instead, in order to stop a vice, we must look to how we can reduce stress levels.

Do we know the original cause of the behaviour?

What is your horse's environment like?

Is he in pain?

Does he have ad lib forage?

Have ulcers and other pain related issues all been ruled out?

Is he a generally anxious personality?

Is he being turned out enough?

What is his back ground, experiences and past emotional state like?

Does he have company?

Is he being bullied by other herd members?

Has anything recently changed around the time of the onset of the vice?

Ideally we need to rule out any issues within the above list. It may be that something as simple as changing your horse's diet, providing him with more forage, turning him out for longer, or replacing a stable with a field shelter to enable him to stay out more, will help him. In some cases changes such as these, can be enough to change a newly formed vice. In the case of habitual or long standing vices, the horse may even be unaware of his own behaviour, as it has become so engrained that it is now automatic to him. You could liken this to someone drumming their fingers on a desk or table, or biting their nails when watching the television. Often people are not aware of what they are doing when they have reinforced this habit over a ling period of time, until it is pointed out to them.

Once we have made all of the obvious positive changes that we can and we are still seeing not only the vice, but that the cause of it - the stress is still remaining. Even after physical pain and ulcers have been definitively ruled out, it is then time to look a little more deeply into things.

The next step available to you in helping your horse, that is well worth trying is, various therapies to help with emotional discord. These may come in the form of flower essences, the most well known being the Bach Flower Remedies.

Personally my preferred therapy in instances such as these would be Zoopharmacognosy, also known as Equine Aromatics. In this therapy the horse is offered different plant matter in the form of powders and essential oils, as well as others. Due to his sensitive olfactory system and innate knowledge of medicinal properties of plants, the horse is able to 'self select' his own medications to help with the presenting issues.

More often than not for emotional issues, these will take the form of floral based essential oils.

A word of warning:

Under no circumstances must essential oils be added to a horse's feed. They are extremely strong and potent and just a few drops are detectable in the blood stream, only minutes after the horse has chosen to select them. For this reason oils should only be given and offered to the horse in the correct way by a qualified practitioner, or by someone that is otherwise very knowledgeable as to their toxicity and their contraindications.

I have seen some quite dramatic changes in the emotional state of horses', just through the use of oils alone. For best results I find that the addition of gentle bodywork therapies can complement the changes and aid the horse further.

Amongst those that I have found to be beneficial to the horse in circumstances such as these are:

 Bowen Therapy, Equine Touch and the Masterson Method.

More information on these therapies and a list of practitioners in your area, can be found on the internet. Basically, the more we can help our horse to relax, the less likely he will be to carry on with his vice. As the emotional need for it, the blocking of his emotional issues, or inability to deal with them, will no longer be needed, as he is feeling safe and secure in himself and his surroundings.

If we find ourselves in the situation where everything has been ruled out pain wise and that the horse is showing no signs of stress and anxiety. It may well then be that the issue of one of a habitual vice. In the instance of cribbing or wind-sucking, you could then try setting up and running another fence a few feet away from your existing one. If you find that your horse is not distressed due to not being able to get to the fence and fence posts to crib or wind-suck. Then it may be the case that after a period of time, the habitual vice starts to fade, in regards to your horse feeling the need to carry out the physical act.

The bottom line is, that whilst we are evaluating a vice and arranging which course of action we are needing to take, to help our horse. We must not try and forcibly stop the vice - for the reasons I have explained above. To do so could cause an escalation of stress and anxiety for your horse. Although annoying, it is better to put up with renewing a few fence rails whilst we are sorting things out, than causing our horse emotional and mental harm.

Although not considered by some to strictly fall into the category of vices. I also feel it is important to discuss the subject of horses self harming. Although not common place, self harming is by no means rare either. Most often it is seen in stallions that are stabled for long periods of time and find themselves therefore, in a very stressful situation. However it is not strictly limited to stallions and may manifest in any horse, that is suffering from extreme stress, frustration or anger. Rather than act out behaviour outwardly, the self harmer will instead, turn his anger or frustration and stress inward on himself.

Typical types of self harming may display themselves in the form of the horse biting himself, repeatedly banging his legs against a fence or door until his knees bleed, or repeatedly banging his head against objects. Should self harming been seen in a horse it should be taken *very* seriously. Not only can it lead to serious injury for the horse, but a change in the behaviour could result in serious injury for the handler also. A horse that is displaying self harm, is a horse that is seriously stressed and unable to cope or release his emotional discord in other ways. In the case of self harming it is also extremely important to also rule out deep rooted pain. Any suspicion of a horse self harming, must be acted upon *immediately* and the cause and remedy for it looked into without hesitation.

As with vices, simply trying to prevent the behaviour is not enough and may escalate the emotional issues further, causing the horse to want to self harm. The owner should look to what is causing the behaviour and mental anguish. What can be changed to try and ease it? Again the therapies that I have already mentioned should be beneficial to the horse and are well worth trying.

Placing the horse in an environment that he is less likely to be able to injure him self on things, will also be of benefit for his physical safety. Please do not let the behaviour continue, or you will be risking both yourself and your horse further stress and physical harm.

In cases such as these, it is also wise to seek out a qualified behaviourist to help you. As it may be the case that they are able to spot any subtle clues that you are as an owner are missing. Veterinary advice should also be one of the first things on your list to rule out the behaviour being caused by pain – don't delay.

HOW OUR HORSES PERCIEVE US

We are predators - hunters and our eyes are set on the sides of our heads; staring eyes of a hunter.

These physical characteristics we may not be able to change, but by softening our other elements such as our energy, our stare, breathing and body language and even the way we think and perceive, we can change the way we are viewed by these magnificent prey animals.

In their wisdom, horses will search for all of the elements of our being, enabling them to form an overall image of how we look and more importantly, how we feel to them. How we choose to express these elements will have a dramatic effect on the horse and their desire to be in our company or not. We will affect their emotional state minute by minute, dependent on our presentation. Our underlying subtle signals we are giving off, give an impression of who we are to the horse, in that moment.

Horses are sentient beings; they feel in just the same way as we do, in many cases being even more sensitive than humans. This is due to their innate prey instinct and connection with the earth and with nature. They have learnt to survive over many years by way of their senses. They have ability to feel the pressure changes in atmosphere, chemical changes both in the air and in individuals. As well as electromagnet energy and other naturally occurring energies such as ley-lines (the earth's natural meridian lines and earth energies) and accident black spots.

To fully understand this, we only have to cast our minds back to the tsunami. It was reported that before the event was known of, animals made their way to higher ground, due to their senses and the change in energy and atmosphere, that pre-warned them through their senses.

So is it of any wonder that how we are feeling, thinking and the atmosphere that we emit is of major importance to our horse?

If we have just had an argument with someone, or we are feeling frustrated, our energy with be heightened and feel 'prickly' to our horse. Likely it will put them on edge and make us feel less inviting to be with. If our horse is one of a more sensitive nature, this may cause him react by removing himself of our space. He may be more alert and unable to focus, as well as feeling anxious. If we are just about to start a schooling session, both ours and our horse's focus will be lessened. Neither will be able to fully concentrate, or make the connection with the other in the way that it is needed. Mistakes may occur; snowballing the frustration of both parties, we are setting both our self and our horse to fail.

If we are feeling depressed, our energy will be low and muggy; our horse will feel lethargic, may lack physical energy and feel pulled down in our company. It is unfair of us to go to our horse when we feel this way, just as much as it is unfair to put on a false smile, in a bid to con them into thinking that we are feeling alright. For this reason alone we owe it to not only ourselves, but also our horse to remain as grounded, focused and balanced as we can be. If we want our relationship to work well, we must be with our horse in a way that creates the best energetic and emotional environment possible. When we choose to try and hide our depression, or our anxiety behind a false smile. The chemical changes of our emotional estate, the energy of it and our body language will give the game away. Our horse is then being bombard by a multitude of conflicting emotions that, they will have a problem with trying to decipher, due to the lack of consistency within those emotions and signals.

Grounding is such an important part of being with our horse. When we are grounded we are focused on the here and now, instead of our body being present with our horse, but our mind being else where. It enables our horse to see and feel how we are at that moment in time. When we are grounded, we are thinking and feeling as our authentic self and this will create positive changes in our body language. No conflicting signs will be sent out and our horse will be able to read us correctly. Grounding will also aid our body in being able to relax. In the case of riding, we will have a focused mind, relaxed seat and our body will more naturally be able to move in rhythm with the horse.

When we approach our horse with an anxious mind, that then also reflects within our energy and body language the inner anxiety that we are feeling; our horse will feel unsettled. Our movements even if we are unaware, will be sharper and quicker and our body not as fluid. Our heart rate will be higher than normal, as well as our breath rate being increased. Added to this is our brainwave state, our brainwaves will register a more alert state that will cause the horse to synchronise with them. We will likely not be breathing properly and at times we are even holding our breath in. It may even be that when we speak to our horse verbally, our pitch will be higher and the words will come faster and more bluntly, lacking softness.

Imagine if you will, sitting in a field with the sun on your back. Minding your own business, happy and exploring the sights and smells and other stimuli within your environment. Your body is relaxed, your breathing is deep and slow and you are feeling content. Up then walks a horse and stands before you. His nostrils flared; his breathing escalates invading your person space, there is no pause or request to enter.

He stands and barges you with his nose and then looks at you with wide eyes. He fidgets where he stands; he is unsettled.

How does he make you feel?

How has the environment and atmosphere changed?

How is this having an effect on your emotional state?

Has you body changed?

Has it become more alert?

Has your heart rate increased?

Are you holding your breath?

Now let us go back to our balanced state again - breathing, relaxed and grounded. Let us now invite in the relaxed horse, the one that is balanced in mind and body and grounded in the moment.

How is your body changing now?

Is it in fact changing at all?

If there is change, this time is it a positive one?

Maybe this time your breathing slows further?

Maybe your heart opens and you feel willing and able to fully invite the horse into your space without question?

I hope that the above exercise has worked for you. It is such a simple one and yet it speaks volumes. It enables us to experience as the horse does, as indeed these experiences are not just limited to us as humans. Please revisit this exercise often; your horse will thank you for it, as you learn to adapt yourself easily. This will aid his life and relationship with you and will be of mutual benefit for both parties.

Your observations of how your horse reacts in your company and that of others, as well as their interactions with other herd members, will no doubt have been noted. Each personality that enters into the space of another will have a dramatic effect on both parties.

Imagine if you will the emotion of anxiety. Then recall how it feels when someone open and calm in mind and body enters into your space.

How does that change you?

So many horses have lived stressful lives, or at the very least have been forced to engage in stressful encounters in the form of humans, or other horses.

When we encounter a horse that is displaying anxiety, there are two different ways that we can greet them. The first is to go straight to them as we are. This will likely cause our brainwaves to synchronise with their own and our heart rate increase along with our breathing rate. We have reached the same state as the horse and it becomes the blind leading the blind; no one party is of any use to the other.

Rather, let us stand back a moment - take a deep breathe and be aware that they may make a sudden movement and not be happy for us to enter into their space straight away. Their heightened state will cause them to take a little longer to assess us, as they will likely be not just surveying us, but also their focus will be split between all of the other potential threats that are also within their immediate environment. Let us pause for a few moments - let us give them time to satisfy themselves that what else is going on

111

around them, the sights, the smells and the atmosphere are all safe enough for them to disconnect their focus from. This will enable them to shift their focus onto us fully. To do this our shoulders must be relaxed, we must turn our eyes away so as to not make direct eye contact and not enter into our predator mode. We need to slow our breathing and allow our heart rate to drop. We must be aware of any tension that we hold in our body, as the horse will see and feel it.

Try breathing out a few times and wait for the horse to show signs of release. This may be shown in the form of yawning, a breath out, shifting from one back leg to the other, licking and chewing, or the lowering of the head. Once one or more of these are seen, you have enabled the horse to relax in our company. It is now safe for us to enter into his space. Without making eye contact, move to his shoulder where he can still see you. Remain relaxed and offer an out stretched hand towards him, palm down. Do not pat him! Horses are exceptionally sensitive to touch and the hard touch of a slap or pat, along with the soft touch of a pesky fly can be just as annoying and worrying. Instead, offer him a firm but at the same time, gentle touch when you feel the time is right. Then breathe out and wait for his next sign of release. Once this is seen it is a sure sign that he is synchronising with us in a way that will enable him to relax to varying degrees. This can only be of benefit to him and indeed your relationship with him, in this moment in time.

He has enabled you to enter his space and in doing so in such a manner, given you his permission and welcomed you - what an honour!

So what do horses associate us with?

The answers to this question are numerous and I have no doubt that the readers of this book will arrive at their own answers. However, to get the ball rolling, I will introduce a few ideas you may not have thought of. Not only to give you ideas, but also to show the vast array of answers, some you may not even have considered.

Being ridden

Pain

Comfort

Excitement

Stress

Food

Touch

Anxiety

Sensory stimulation

Security

Encouragement

Partnership

His tack

Torture

Confidence

Your actions, thoughts, feelings and how you approach and touch your horse, as well as your behaviour towards him - will be the deciding factor in how he views you. You alone can make it uncomfortable or a joy for him to have you around.

Due to the majority of the readers of this book being riders. I can not express enough the importance and need to cover the subject of riding in this chapter. What we have considered and taken on aboard is just as important in the saddle, as it is on the ground, if not more so. When we are sat on our horse and not stood at his side. We are giving him the added status of 'the leader that helps keeps us both safe'. Whilst to a degree this is a role covered by both horse and rider, the horse is the one 'upfront', taking instruction from his co-pilot 'behind'. He is the one with his feet on the floor and he is the one who has the over riding decision on how fast you move and to where to. No matter how much those reins may pull to instruct other wise. It is for this reason that a true connection needs to be in place. Without this connection the focus between horse and rider can not be fully present. We need to be 'mindful' rather than 'mind full'.

I was contacted by a client around six years ago. She and her horse were to compete at HOYS. The reason that she contacted me was that she was worried over the fact that her horse was not working for her in the way she felt he should be.

She was felt that he was 'holding back'. This was causing confusion for her, as she felt she was riding him no differently to usual and he was still working fine with other people.

I asked her how she felt about riding him at HOYS. Her reply was 'I am shit scared'. I asked her if this thought passed through her mind whilst she was riding him - she replied that it did. She told me that sometimes she would feel frustrated and tell him that if he did not work properly for her, she would send him to the pie factory. During the time she had these thoughts he responded well to her cues and there appeared to be no issue.

The answer was clear; it was simply an issue with mixed signals that she was sending out to her horse. During the time she was riding and thinking of how she felt about riding at HOYS, her heart rate was increasing, as was her breathing. Subconsciously she was further holding her horse back by applying tension to the reins, as a way of stopping him moving forwards. If they did not work well together, they would not be able to attend - equalling no stress. So why would she actually be wanting him to perform well in his ridden work with her, if it would only lead to a stressful event? After all, failing would be far less stressful! So here we have found our first answer – inner fear.

So what then was it about the pie factory threats *(of course this was only a thought and she never had any intention of carrying it through)* that caused him to work correctly with her? These thoughts came during the time when she was feeling confident and driving her horse forwards instead of holding him back. He was simply reading her body language during both of these mind states and giving her exactly what she was asking for each time. What a clever horse! There was of course no issue with him whatsoever. He just had the ability to read all of the instructions and cues being offered, rather than being selective.

I do not know if they made it to HOYS, but after we found the answer to these problems, I advised the lady on several exercises that she could use to help herself that I know work well. If they did go and she used my exercises as described, I have no doubt that they will have done well.

Another of my clients had a point to pointer. She was having issues with her horse when each race began. Instead of starting off quickly as the other horses did. He always held back as if waiting for the others to go out in front so that he could follow their lead, or so his rider thought.

Again as we chatted about how she felt, the point was raised that she was afraid of jumping - she liked it, but she feared it at the same time. She was due to race again the following week. That time she did well. This undoubtedly was down to the fact that she had acknowledged her fear, found her courage and was no longer sending her horse the cues for 'please do not start the race'. As of course, what had been playing out before was that at the start of the race, she was asking him to hold back. She had then seen the other horses out in front, worried and given him the instruction to get moving.

As the above stories show only too well, our horses do not just pick up on the instruction and cues we offer physically and consciously, but also the ones that are subconscious and cause our physical bodies to subtlety back up those thoughts. Always remain 'mindful' of what you are truly thinking or feeling, adjust your thought, breathing and body tension accordingly. Be sure that what you want your horse to hear is actually correct and not in conflict with what you think and feel. Your horse knows what you are saying, he always does.

You can't con him into thinking otherwise.

GROUNDWORK

Without a doubt groundwork is the under pinning foundation of everything we do with out horses.

If we can not even ask our horse to lead properly, how do we expect to be able to ride him correctly? A foal's basic training should always include haltering, leading and the lifting of feet. By helping them learn these things from an early age, should their be an emergency, we stand a much better chance of them being able to remain calm when handled and in need of help.

Problems can arise when horses have not had their early training put in place, or that it has been put in place incorrectly. Sadly over the years I have come across no end of stories of foals strangling themselves, through being tied up and left to 'pull back'. Also stories of horses in their teens, that are still not able to stand still when tied without worrying. By allowing a foal to pull back in such a way against a solid object, we risk long term injury of the poll area of the head. It is not uncommon for horses in later life to still have physical longer term issues with their poll, due to their experiences in their early years.

When we lead a horse, the horse should be at our shoulder or behind our shoulder. Horses that tend to try and walk out in front of us, are those that have either not been taught to lead correctly, or those of a stressful nature. When we allow the horse to walk out in front of us, should they suddenly be startled and run. We are at much more risk of them running in front of us and tripping us, or pulling us over. If a horse is walking out in front of us, his focus is also more likely to be on his surroundings rather than on us. In the event that they are started they will choose to look ahead, rather than to us for instruction.

Lifting Feet

When a horse lifts his feet on request his comfort is power-mount. Many horses have issues with varying degrees of lameness, which may not be apparent to us when we see them walking. This may show itself as reluctance to lift a hoof, as this will mean putting more weight onto the hoof that is sore or the leg or shoulder further up. Any reluctance to lift one hoof, whilst being happy to lift the opposite one, should be taken notice of.

Sacrum issues in horses are more common than we may first expect. Whilst a horse may look 'sound' in his movement, it may be that the issues and pain only arise when the horse is asked to lift his hind leg, due to him having to contract the muscles that may be uncomfortable for him. Couple this with the fact that too many Farriers choose to lift horse's hind legs to high, as well as pulling them out to the side, and it is all too easy to see why so many horses that have problems and are reluctant. Wobblers Syndrome can be another cause of reluctance to lift the hind legs. Wobblers Syndrome is where there is a nerve issue within the spinal column. When the hind leg is lifted, the nerve is pressed and the muscles are compromised and unable to (fire) contract and de-contract as needed. This will result in the characteristic 'wobble' of the hind leg, or hind end of the horse. Due to this causing the horse to feel unsteady, he may not feel safe offering and holding up his hind leg for you.

Issues can also arise through expectant pain. If the horse knows that holding his leg up may be painful, it may make him hold it up too high which can cause added pain or the 'wobble'. In all cases of leg lifting, it is important that the horse learn that once a leg is lifted, he is able to allow you to take some of the weight for him. By this I do not mean his whole weight and expect you to have to hold him up whilst he leans on you. But part of his weight, to enable him to relax his muscles a little so he does not get stiff and sore. As long as he is over tensing his muscles, he will not feel fully balanced and comfortable and this may cause him to wriggle and pull his leg away from you.

Should a horse that is standing nicely and offering his feet to you, ask for his hoof back, it is likely that all he is asking is to place it on the ground in order that he can rebalance himself. *Is this too much to ask?* He simply wants to be comfortable and do the best he can for you. Let him have his hoof, let him rebalance himself and he will then offer it to you again willingly.

Too many people are willing to argue with horses over holding their feet up. Refusing to let go of them and causing the horse to tense and fall out of balance. Allow him to show you where he is comfortable, to enable him to do his best for you. Show him what is expected of him – explain to him correctly what you are asking him. Most of all reward him when he offers his feet, or lifts them for you on request. Create a situation where he wants to work with you, not fear you, or fear pain and work against you. It is within his benefit to work with you; not against you. If he is not offering you his feet correctly, ask why.

Is he in pain?

Is he feeling unbalanced?

He is scared?

Is he lifting his leg too high and unbalancing himself?

Is he lame?

Do his feet hurt if he stands on a hard surface?

Is he stood unevenly behind?

Is he stood on a hill?

Are you in a bad mood and he can sense it?

Does he trust you and can he trust you?

His feet are his flight....

There is a school of thought that tells us to hold on to the horses foot when he tries to take it away, and only to give it back to him once he stands still. What it fails to take into account is that he may be in pain, unbalanced and unable to stand still. Holding onto his hoof in such a way may only breed resentment, concern and cause a lack of trust and pain. Instead, let him know if he needs his foot, or if he is worried he can have it. Once he comes to understand this and is rewarded for offering it to you, he will have no concern over handing it to you. Use logic, think like your horse and respect him. He will always have his reasons for not responding in the way you are expecting. Your role as his care taker is to find out the 'why'.

Leading At Liberty

There will be times when a head collar and lead rope are not always to hand and we need to move our horse. For this reason, as well as the beauty of liberty, it is always good to teach a horse to lead without. In fact leading at liberty is an excellent way to first teach foals to lead. Once they have learnt to lead in this way, a head collar will almost be invisible to them and us, as it is not needed and only really there for safety and as a precaution. Helping them to lead in such away will also prevent any possible damage caused by them pulling back. The simple teaching of 'walk on' and 'whoa' and rewarding them when they listen and respond well to our instruction, will often be enough for them to understand and lead nicely. Then once a head collar is applied there will be little if any issue for it.

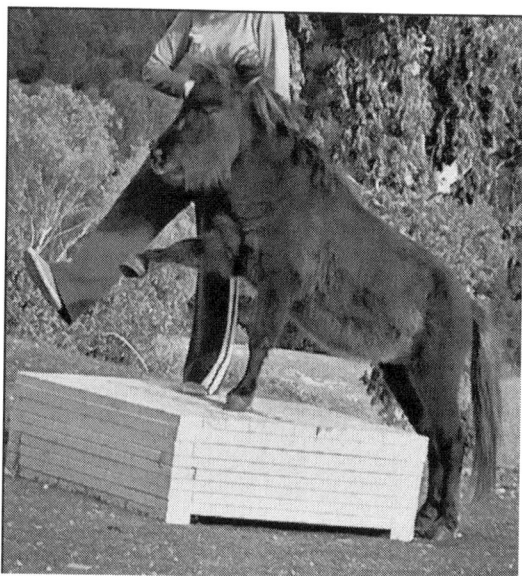

When first teaching to lead at liberty, if you are finding that your horse starts to wander a little. You may like to try starting off with a lead rope loose around their neck. Caution must be taken that the horse does not run off like this and get himself caught up. The idea is not to lead him by the rope, but rather, just to use the rope to regain his focus if his attention starts to wander. Each time he brings his focus back to you, rewarding him for his correct response and asking him to 'walk on' again. Once he understands, the rope may be removed and you are working together beautifully in liberty, through his choice to want to be with you.

The above techniques are the foundation of almost everything you do with your horse. Each of these techniques can be adapted to fit in with whatever you are asking of your horse.

Always remember; correct response equals reward.

Create his desire to want to work with you and respect him for what he so graciously offers you in return.

Once we have the foundations laid and our horse is responding nicely and listening to request. He is able to engage in full focus with us. We are now ready to move into the saddle where we can continue his education.

TRAILER LOADING

There are many different techniques that are used for loading a horse onto a trailer or lorry; the safe and the not so safe. When loading a horse, it is of utmost importance that it is done not only in the way that is safest for both you and the horse, but also in a way that is likely to create the best possible outcome mentally for the horse. This means that when he is presented with the trailer the next time, he will have little or no fear of entering it.

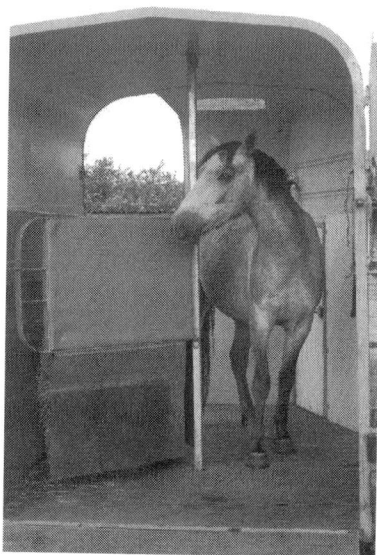

Many of you will be familiar with one of the most common trailer loading methods used today. This technique is based on the idea that in order to make the horse move forwards when refusing to do so. We must make it more uncomfortable for him move backwards. Thereby creating a pattern of recall based on instinctual survival and self preservation. As well as trying to relieve and move away from the physical and mental pressure, that is being applied by the handler.

Put in simple terms it is the training of, 'it is more comfortable and doesn't' 'hurt', if you move forwards when asked'. Being a prey animal it is easy to see why a disorientated and scared horse may give in to these crude techniques. This will be due to his looking for a safe corner in which to submit in. He wants and needs the mental and physical discomforts go away. An important consideration is that it does not remove the cause of the refusal that was there in the first place. Rather, it masks it with a bigger fear, the fear of physical discomfort and inflicted or perceived harm. For that moment in time the biggest thing on the horse's mind is survival and what it can do to survive - so he complies.

He has been brainwashed into doing exactly what is desired of him. He wants to relieve the pressure and is unable to think of another way. So the idea of 'when in doubt do this', comes into play right on cue and as expected. That is until a well orientated horse that refuses to be bullied, comes a long. This horse won't load with this methodology; or at least it will be difficult to load him. He is far too mentally well integrated and will not be bullied. This is where this method fails. The horse is not loading of his own free will and in confidence, so when he is of free mind he is aware of the need to make a decision. His decision is that he will not be bullied.

Further to this in my work with horses. I have come across no end of reasons for refusal to load.

The two most worrying ones being:

Horses that became aware on their last journey that the lorry or trailer floor was not safe, or that the loading ramp was unstable.

There are also a huge amount of horses with slow muscular responses, due to the electrical signals not being passed in the brain or through the spinal column quickly enough. This can be seen in the case of a 'wobbler', but it is also a problem for a huge number of horses that do not show a physical 'wobble' and appear fine on firm ground and in movement. It is not until the unnatural extra effort needed for balancing on a moving object in this way, that the slow reaction of the muscles contracting becomes a problem. When this happens the horse is unable to brace itself quickly enough to balance safely.

For these two reasons alone a horse should not be forced onto a trailer without there having been strictly carried out checks. As to fail to do so, is putting the horse's life at risk. You could end up with a horse that ends up with his legs through the floor, having them dragged along the road in transit - or a horse that ends up downed in the trailer or lorry as he has fallen, unable to keep his balance. These are only two reasons why a horse can refuse to load. There are many more reasons also, so maybe we should be looking into these reasons instead of using mental and physical force. Force for any reason other than in the case of a major medical or life threatening emergency is not only disrespectful to our equine friends, in some cases it can cause a fatal outcome.

Let us take for an example a typical scenario of a horse that has always loaded well and now is refusing.

Where do we start?

What questions need to be raised?

Has the horse loaded onto this same lorry or trailer before?

If the answer is 'yes' and if there was no issue previously, then maybe the trailer or lorry has an issue and needs to be checked.

Has the horse had an accident since?

Even an accident in the field?

Is the horse showing anything abnormal in their movement, however slight?

Has your horse suffered from any health issues lately?

Is your horse elderly and not as free moving as he once was?

Did the last trailer loading and journey go smoothly?

Where they travelled alone or in company?

If travelled with a friend that they got along with, are they being travelled with the same friend?

Is the intention to travel them alone which they are not used to?

With a companion they do not know or do not get along with?

What happened last time when they were unloaded at the other end?

If the answer is 'no', do you know how they loaded previously onto other vehicles?

In fact, have they ever even been loaded before?

If they have loaded previously with little or no issue, then what has changed this time?

Are you asking them to load onto a trailer when last time it was a lorry?

Where they loaded by a different handler?

Loaded with a friend on board first?

Loaded with a friend close by and alone now?

Do they look concerned?

Do they just look disinterested?

What happened last time when they reached their destination?

Does the lorry or trailer look dark and uninviting?

If so, it may be that no one has considered to open the front ramps or doors to let in more light (if safe to do so).

These are just many of the different questions that we need to be asking ourselves, when our horses are refusing to load. It is all very well getting them on there by using any method that works, but if we want them to reach their destination safely and without issue. Then the way in which we load them and how they feel about that experience is of huge importance. We do not want to risk reaching our destination with a dead horse, due to our failure to listen to them.

When being loaded onto a trailer, the horse should always be consulted and worked with as a willing partner, with their feelings and concerns surrounding the event being taken into consideration. From the first time a horse loads, a memory will be created that will stay with them. If that memory is an unpleasant one, then not only have we by use of force made it that way, but we have also caused concern for them in regard to any future loadings.

We need to set the horse up in a positive way and enable him the best stress free and comfortable experience that we are able to. Not only will this make life easier for him, but for us also. There is little more frustrating than wanting to load our horse to take them to a nice place. Where we can enjoy and experience together. Only to have it turn sour right from the beginning through having to use pressure and force to even get to our destination.

Ideally from the first time your horse is loaded it will have been done correctly. The horse will have been given time to explore the vehicle, with both the ramp up and down. He will have not been rushed and the sensible owner will have created positive association with the vehicle. This may come in a reward of some kind such as food, or a good scratch each time the horse has shown positive interest in it.

A food bucket may have been put on the ramp and then moved further into the vehicle, as the horse slowly makes his way up and ramp and inside to explore. When the horse has taken steps backwards, I hope that he will have been allowed to do so. It is just his way of making sure he can and that he will not become 'stuck' in there.

Has he previously been loaded with a lunge line around his back end? Maybe he is not walking forward because it has become ingrained within his psyche that he should load only once the lunge line touches his rear end? Maybe he is not refusing, maybe he is just waiting for his known cue he knows and you don't.

Could it be that the previous time he stepped on to the ramp it was by accident, as he shuffled his feet about, enabling his first hoof to find its way on?

Does he actually even know how that happened?

Does he even know that he has to lift his leg to step on?

Maybe he is just needing your help and to be shown how?

Help make it a pleasurable experience for him, to enable you to go out together and enjoy. The last thing both you and your horse need in an emergency situation is a horse that refuses to load, due to his past experiences not being comfortable and productive for him.

The first time you load him, do not just close the doors behind him and move off. Instead, days before give him time to explore, park up your trailer or lorry and leave all ramps down. Allow him to load on and off so that he can experience that he can do so safely. Let him know he is not stuck and has no need to be afraid of being trapped. The trailer and lorry where never designed to be an instrument of mental torture, but sadly through the training some horses have experienced, this is exactly what the trailer has become. We can change that for them. It just takes time, thought, consideration and patience on our part.

Let us consider our horses and understand them in the best way we can. Let us set them up to win and be confident. It will be of benefit to all in the long run.

RIDDEN EDUCATION

The age that we choose to begin ridden education with our horses is of extreme importance. Too many people are in a rush to do this, invading their horse at an age where they are still mentally and physically immature. Even a horse that appears to have filled out and achieved his full height can still be physically immature. This is due to the immature structure of his body in the form of his skeletal frame, that may as not yet be ready and strong enough to carry the weight of a rider. He also may not yet have developed the relevant stomach muscles and top line needed, that enables him to hold his back correctly to support the weight of a rider.

Personally I prefer a horse to be five years old or better still older, before I will consider backing him. This allows the time needed for him to mature in all ways that he needs too. Especially as some of his growth plates may not fully be developed until he is the age of seven in some breeds. With so much fun on the ground and liberty training available to us, there is no need to rush him before he is ready. Enjoy him whilst he is young and lay his training foundations wisely. As this is sure to pay off once his ridden education begins.

The process we work through in the horse's ground training is of upmost importance and if done correctly, his 'backing' should go without any fuss at all. Unless there are other underlying factors, that need to be taken into consideration for the individual. With his ground training in place correctly, he has come to trust you and in that, your judgment also. Take it steady, take your time, he will thank you for it and it will aid in a successful and stress free experience for you both.

Preparation

Firstly, it is important that our horse knows how to stand on request, walk on and whoa (stop). All of these things you will have covered within your groundwork. Make sure you horse is relaxed when responding to your requests, that he is focused on you and what you are asking to enable him to be consistent and gain reward.

It may also be worth considering long lining him and helping him learn this technique. This will enable him to build confidence and work from further cues.

Introducing the Saddle

It is common place for an old saddle to be used. A saddle that is just kept for backing horses, as a way of making sure the better and expensive saddles are not damaged. This is all well and good, but if we are backing a horse it is no good putting something onto his back and then adding weight to it, if it is not comfortable for him. It is a little like putting ill fitting shoes on a toddler and expecting him to take his first steps in them to save scuffing his best ones. However, an old saddle is useful for putting on the floor and hanging over the fence to enable the horse to explore it in his own way. Whether that be sniffing, pawing or standing on it - let him have a good play with it.

It is always good to enable him to get used to his saddle cloth first. Being as it is soft and easy to rub over his body and easy for him to explore on the floor without it being damaged. Many people tend to wash saddle clothes in fabric softener and other highly floral smelling chemicals. Not only can these smells be confusing for the horse, but some horses will also react to the washing powders in the form of allergic reaction. Keeping you saddle cloth as horse friendly as you can is important, as it will later come into close contact with his body. He has to feel safe and comfortable with it.

Once the introduction it has been made, ask him if you can rub it over his body, across his back and up his neck. Allow him to move away and sniff and turn to face to it if he feels the need. Wait for his permission for the touch to take place. Not only will this help him get used to the feeling of the cloth being moved over his body in preparation for tacking up, but it will also now be covered in his scent. This will make it familiar the next time he encounters it.

Next we have the saddle, once he has accepted his saddle and 'met it'. It is now time to introduce it onto his back. First stand with him, just holding it and allow him to sniff it. If he moves away, or does anything else he feels he needs to do by way of his response, just read his body language and respond accordingly.

What is he saying to you?

Is he telling you he is unsure?

That he is ready for it to come closer?

That he has no concerns over what you are holding in your hands?

Once you are sure that he is feeling comfortable. Gently lower the saddle onto his back and keep hold of it. He may tense a little, just reassure him and talk to him gently. Should he tense too much and choose to move forwards, allow him to do so as you lift the saddle to enable him to move forwards without concern. Watch out for his signs of acceptance and relaxation and reward him as soon as they are seen. If he is still looking comfortable, gently lift the saddle - take it to one side again. Reward him for standing still and put it onto his back again.

If he is still looking happy to continue, you may tighten the girth very gently, pausing if you should see him tense. It does not need to be done up fully, just enough that should he react his saddle will not slip to the side and startle him. Each time you see him relax, reward him and then ask him to walk along side you, again rewarding him for his correct response.

Lesson one is now complete; in fact for me that is the lesson for the day. Other than taking him for a walk in his saddle, I would not personally be asking more from him on day one. Look how far he has come already! Instead, I would repeat the process the following day and if he still appears comfortable, I would then lead onto his bridling.

Introducing the Bridle

When backing a horse I like to use the least invasive equipment that I can. So for me my first choice is always a Side-pull bitless bridle, or a plain head collar. If the horse is being backed properly and in his own time, then there should be no use for anything more. If his attention is on you and you have created an environment of trust, he has no need to be worried or have his attention on what else is going on around him. If he has, then this may well indicate his concern and that he is not yet ready. He may need more groundwork to be done, to enable him to feel more secure within the process, or the quiet repeating but not nagging of the experience.

Mounting

Before we even consider mounting we need to make sure the environment is correct, so should the unexpected happen and our horse suddenly moves and cause us to fall, neither party will be hurt.

Ideally you will have already gotten your horse used to having you lean your weight over his back to some degree, with little or no reaction.

Show him the solid object that you intend to stand on. Let him sniff it and get used to it, so that he is happy to stand along side it. Ask him to stand, reward him for doing so. Then lead him to it, asking him to stand - then offer the reward when he calmly does as asked. All the time this is going on be aware of your own breathing. Make sure you are not holding your breath and that you are breathing deeply, checking that your body is not tense.

Now stand on the mounting block, ask him to stand by you and reward him again. Put your hands on the saddle and apply a little pressure to enable him to feel the weight. Reward him for staying, ignoring him if he moves slightly, then reward him as he stands and relaxes again. Once he appears happy and comfortable with what you are doing. Try your leg over his saddle and then pause and breathe out.

What is he doing?

Is he remaining still?

Is he tensing a leg as if to move?

Has he turned to look at you?

If he tenses remove your leg. Wait for him to relax again and then reward him. Once you see the relaxation from him, try again, always remembering to breathe out first. This time if he remains calm and still, try moving yourself into the saddle gently and without wriggling. He may now choose to move forwards, that is alright – he is just trying it out.

Go for a little walk with him, only a few minutes

if he is happy with it. Be aware he may feel the need to explore how this new weight feels on his back by shaking. If he does just hold onto the saddle. Don't forget as he walks to keep rewarding him, he is offering you what you are asking for. Ask for a 'Whoa' and reward him when he stops.

When the horse is ready and willing and all of the ground preparation has been out in - it literally can be as simple as this. No lunging, no running round a round-pen, no wearing him out first. Just good solid trust and respect on both sides.

Breathing is the key to everything within this process. It is the sign you can offer to your horse, to enable him to know you are not scared and he has no need to be either. By breathing out and breathing deeply you are encouraging him to do the same.

FEEDING FOR HEALTH

It is a sad fact that much of the land that horses graze on and their hay is cut from, is lacking in valuable nutrition that is much needed in their diet. If the soil is deficient in the vitamins and minerals needed, then so will the grazing be. This may have come about through the field being overly grazed in the past, the soil being too acidic or too alkaline, or just general poor land management.

There are various PH tests to checks available, to help you establish if you soil is too acidic or too alkaline. Many tests will also be able to check for mineral levels and content of your soil, as well as testing forage. The best place to find out about these tests if your local farmers Co-op or feed company.

If your tests show that your soil is deficient, the company will be able to advise you on what you can do about it. The likely advice will be a product to spread on your land. In recent years calcified seaweed was often the product of choice. Due to new dredging laws it is now hard to find in large qualities, but some companies are able to supply alternatives. Last year my own land was too acidic as shown by the characteristic buttercups. The acidity of the soil was also blocking some of the minerals and vitamins needed in the soil. I used a company called Glenside that was able to supply me with a product made of organic lime to help counteract the acidity, and seaweed extract to aid in putting the nutrition back into the soil. Buttercups are poisonous to horses when they are fresh and can lead to photosensitivity in the form of blistering around the nose and mouth. They are safe to consume once they are dried in hay.

What our horse consumes will have an affect on how he feels. Not just in his physical health and energy levels, but due to that how he also feels mentally. When he is deficient in one thing, due to how vitamins and minerals are used by each other to work as they need to. It can cause a break down of the metabolic pathways and lead to malabsorption.

Some examples of this are:

Sodium and potassium are in each cell with a

barrier between them. When one or the other is low, the membrane may become weak leading to 'Leaky Cell Syndrome'. This may lead to pour wound healing, premature ageing and skin issues such mud fever. Vitamin E is also needed in order to aid repair and regeneration of the skin and cells.

Calcium needs vitamin D (absorbed through natural sunlight) and magnesium in order that the body can use it properly.

Iron needs vitamin C in order to be absorbed and used by the body correctly.

Sadly most mineral licks that are on the market and produced for horses are made up of synthetic vitamins and minerals. The body has little use for them and will find it hard to uptake and use them in the way that it needs to. Where possible natural sources of vitamins and minerals should be used, or to a large degree we are wasting our money and not really helping our horse's health in the best way that we can.

Seaweed is an excellent form of electrolytes, vitamins and minerals if you are able to locate a good, well balanced and clean source. My own horses always choose seaweed over any form of salt and mineral blocks. I put some in cold water to soak for ten minutes and then just leave it out for them to help themselves. There is a huge difference in the quantities that they choose to take during hot and cold weather. This shows how different their requirements are during winter and summer months. In summer they will consume a lot more, due to the hotter weather and their need to replenish their electrolytes. A lack of electrolytes or a poor balance of them, can result in filled legs when stabled, as well as swollen sheaths and teats in some cases.

Wood chewing of fences and tress can indicate pain, but can also indicate mineral imbalances, often (but not always) copper. If you see your horse regularly chewing wood it is well worth ruling out the issue of pain and then looking towards his nutrition.

Due to our horses living and grazing on the same land for years, the use of fencing to create safe boundaries is imporant. Hedges where possible are preferable to fencing. Not only do hedges provide better shelter from the elements, but they can also provide important medicines and nutrition. Horses to a large degree have lost their choice to be able to roam to find the plants needed, in order to self medicate and give them correct nutrition. Often what we see as weeds; nettles, dandelions and thistles for instance, are a valuable source required by the horse.

Dandelions – diuretic and helps to support liver and kidneys.

Thistles – helps to cleanse the liver.

Nettles - a good source of iron and a general blood tonic.

Plantain- (hook-weed) - anti bacterial, anti inflammatory and topically helps relieve itching of skin and bites.

Hawthorn - helps relieve pain, improves circulation and helps to lower blood sugar levels.

Elderflower - anti septic, anti inflammatory, respiratory issues and reduces blood sugar levels.

Rosehips - a great source of vitamin C and beta carotenes.

Hazel - helps with pain, inflammation and mucus.

Ash - a bitter tonic and astringent, laxative and an anti inflammatory.

Willow – helps to reduce fever, pain and inflammation.

Cleavers (sticky bud) - diuretic, helps clean the blood, helps to lower blood pressure and is an anti inflammatory.

Meadowsweet - can help with ulcers, inflammation and mucus.

If the trees that your horse is interested in are too high, just cut down a few branches and leave them on the floor. It will not be long before you find they have been stripped of their bark and leaves. Please keep in mind that some trees such as sycamore and yew are highly toxic to horses and should be removed from their environment.

Often what we consider weeds, are in fact medicine for our horses. There is nothing more beautiful than a quiet walk inhand on a lovely day with your horse. Allowing him to stop, sniff and choose his own medications and nutritional needs along the hedge rows. Not only is it a good way of helping your horse to help himself. It also enables you to spend some quality time together. Just watching him and what he chooses to select and consume is educational in itself. If we are short of time, just ten minutes out on a brisk walk with a bucket is all that is needed in order to harvest some healthy goodies to bring home to him.

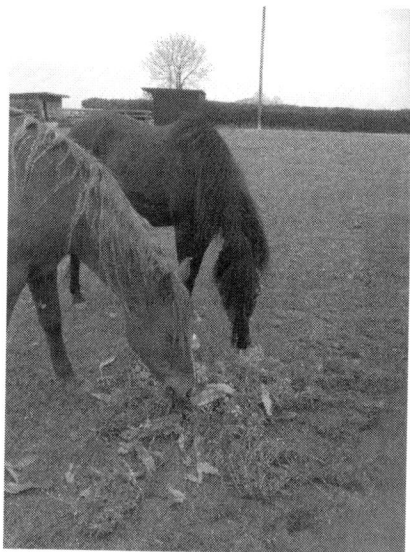

Many of these plants die back in winter when the horse's immune system may be lower and his nutritional needs may be higher. It is good practice to collect then during the summer months or early autumn and dry them out. You can put them into breathable bags and keeping them dry to enable them to be available to your horse as and when needed.

Processed Feeds

With the large array of products on the market along with their fancy advertising, knowing what to feed can be some what of a nightmare. Most of these feeds will contain Recommended Daily Allowance (RDA), best suited to the type of feed you are buying. The problem is that how a horse is otherwise being fed will have an impact on his nutritional requirements. RDA is suited to a healthy horse.

What if our horse is lacking in something?

Will RDA then be enough?

When a horse has been deficient in something for along time, once it is reintroduced, chances are the body will not recognise it and uptake it in the same way. Due to this, there will be instances when load dosing is necessary. For this reason, by feeling your horse a standard RDA feed he may not be getting what he needs on a long term basis. Couple this with the fact that many commercial feeds contain nasty chemicals and pesticides and the feeding can lead you on a road to nowhere. Feeds are often bulked out with cereals which horses find hard to digest other than oats. In the wild a horse would choose to consume little if no cereals. It is not part of his natural diet; it is simply a cheap way to bulk out food and mould it into pellets.

Check the Ingredients

What is listed in the side of the bag?

Does the chaff contain bleached straw, molasses to keep the dust down, mould inhibitors and other chemicals?

If I come across any of these ingredients I am afraid the food goes back on the shop shelf. Wherever possible my horses are fed organically. Organic is not a fancy word for expensive as many people think, it means that the food is natural, chemical free and has not been genetically modified. GMO foods are as bad for our horses as they are for us. Studies have shown that they are linked to cancer. Long term feeding of mice with GMO corn resulted in huge tumours. Sadly 80-90% of the world's corn that is produced today is genetically modified.

Our horses are what we feed them; choose their food and nutrition wisely.

If in doubt telephone the company and ask them what the ingredients mean and if it is a comprehensive list. If the company is not willing to openly answer your questions - that in its self may be considered your answer.

Sugarbeet is a common food along with molasses that people are still feeding their horses today. We are told that sugarbeet is a highly digestible fibre that is good for our horses and for bulking out their feeds. However, over the past fifteen years I have found sugarbeet to be the worst culprits for causing food intolerances in horses. This is something I would in no way consider feeding my horses. That is not to say that some horses do not benefit from it and fair well. However, after the cases I have witnessed this is not a chance I would be willing to take, especially with so many suitable foods on the market.

Sugarbeet is sprayed up to 6 times a year with pesticides. Even un-molassed sugarbeet can be as high as 7% in sugar.

Horses all have individual nutritional requirements dependent on the type of land their breed evolved on, as well as their past health, feeding history, their age and their workload. No one food will be suitable for all; though some that contain all of the organic ingredients in the form of all the necessary vitamins, minerals, amino acids etc needed, will be a good starting point....choose wisely.

Ideally we should replace the word 'food' with 'nutrition'.
In other words, are we giving our horse's food or nutrition?

If we are feeding nutrition, then how big the amount of feed in the bowl is, is immaterial. It is the fact that it is good for our horse and meets their requirements that is important. If need be it can always be bulked out with a good source of chaff that is chemical and molasses free.

If in doubt seek the advice of some one that is qualified in natural equine nutrition, rather than one that works for one of the main food companies that use cheap and GMO ingredients. As these are not the best people to advise you on the health of your horse. Instead, choose someone who really cares what goes into the sack and into your horse.

We only have to look back to past generations and back to now, to see just how common Cushings and Equine Metabolic Syndrome have become in recent years. Once thought of as the dis-ease of the old horse, all ages and breeds of horses are now falling prey to it. I have no doubt that this is largely due to the lack of soil condition, repeated spraying of crops, use of synthetic vitamins and minerals in feeds and the heavy processing of our horse feeds used today. All of which our horses are, and never have been, designed to eat.

Let's get our horses back to basics – let's get them healthy and feed them as nature intended.

THE PERSONLITIES AND THE COMPATIABLES

The personalities of horses, their wants, needs and desires are as diverse as we find in humans. Due to this, it stands to reason that not all horses and people will be compatible. Sadly this is one of the many reasons that horses are bought, (sometimes argued with), cause both people and horses to get anxious and many horses to be sold and moved on to new homes.

When we go in search of an equine companion, or make a choice to work with one that belongs to someone else. It is of utmost importance to make the correct decision over the best personality match possible. This enables the relationship whether it is based on companionship, or a working life, to go as smoothly as possible. The other important consideration being that, the chosen horse will also fit in with the herd that he is expected to live in.

Cast your mind back to your school days. The personality of your teacher and how they interacted with you, will have had a huge influence on your willingness and ability to learn the lessons being offered by them.

The sullen dictator that never smiled and made demands of you: Not taking into consideration your own interests and needs and how best you learnt and retained information.

The smiling and 'thinking out of the box' teacher that inspired and nurtured your desire to learn and had the knowledge of how to adapt to each student on a unique level, best suited to the individual. Each personality will have something to offer; but is that offering in the best interests of the individual?

The sullen dictator may have knocked your confidence with their 'no nonsense' approach. Whilst at the same time, the rebellious side of you that was hindering your own progress and ability to listen and perform was aided. This will have helped you to develop the left hand side of your brain, the logical and problem solving side. Whilst the 'thinking out of the box' teacher may have caused you to question further, seek knowledge for yourself, and inspire you to follow your dreams and aided the confidence needed in order to do that. Likely that will have caused you to know that if a question can be answered to 'why?', then another question is needed in order to search for the answers you seek.

This way of teaching will help develop the right hand side of our brain, our ability to visualise, think out of the box, deeply question and enable us to arrive at our own answers. Development of the right side of the brain will also aid our ability to be compassionate and empathise with others - whether they are in a horse or human form.

Both forms of teaching style and approach will have helped within our future relationships. As each style will help will balancing the various sides of the brain. Helping us to create a harmonious approach towards our relationships and our ability to identify with, work with, and think like, each individual that we encounter.

The problem comes when we have only encountered and experienced one style of tutoring in our earlier years. More often than not, this will have had a long lasting effect on how we think, reason and question, as well as how we relate to others. This will in turn have an effect on each and every relationship that we engage in, whether it is horse or human in nature.

Ideally you will have come from a background where you have encountered, endured and enjoyed both teaching styles. This will have aided you in your ability to adapt yourself, to working with different horse personality types. It will have enabled you to empathise with those in need of compassion and extend to them the hand of friendship when fear sets in. As well as being a firm, but fair tutor and leader for those that are rebellious and others find hard to work with through their challenging behaviours.

The Personalities

The Variable

These personalities are never the same each time we encounter them. They may flit between different personality traits. Sometimes faster than some are able to keep up with them. Just as we get used to approaching and working with them in a certain way, they will change their personality and due to that, also their outward behaviour. These types of personalities may also show one behaviour and outward persona to you, only to show another side of them selves when in the presence of others. These horses can also be beneficial as much as they are frustrating (for some). This is due to many such personalities having the ability to fit in with the person or herd that they are with, and adapt themselves accordingly. This may be in the form of the strong, bold cross country horse that revels in the excitement and adrenalin flow of the fast and furious gallop, controlled canter and huge jump. Once a child is put on their back, they breathe out and turn into the quiet plod that is every mothers dream horse and will help to keep the child safe.

Another way in which these horses can benefit certain relationships, or break them, is their ability to change from the calm, quiet and amenable to the wild no nonsense stallion, no matter what their gender. These horses will challenge our mental and emotional ability in a way that will cause us to adapt, keep our cool and relax at the flick of a switch....or break us. Thus, making it clear that this horse is not for us and another personality type is in fact what we need for balance.

An example of how (for some) the variable personality horses can be of benefit, I will use my chestnut Arabian, named Alfi. He was my co-facilitator, or rather my superior, in Equine Facilitated Therapy with clients for several years. His variable personality was perfect for such a task, due to his ability to shift from trait to trait in order to mirror the personality and emotional state of those in his care.

During this time my granddaughter was around four or five. She had two little Miniature Shetland ponies named Meeka and Cinders; her 'cuddle ponies'. They were every little girl's and grandmother's dream. They would happily stand and be pampered and praised, sharing kisses and there was never any concern over accidents occurring. At the time I had several horses. My granddaughter was scared of them, not only because they towered over her, but also due to the fact that Alfi would chase her, ears back and teeth bared, whilst she ran, heart thumping for what she thought was her life. She wanted to like him and feel safe in his company, but she was scared of him and he knew it.

Then one day these worrying displays came to a halt. Alfi was playing out once again, mirroring her fear and the by now typical chase was on. Granddaughter running for what she thought was her life, screaming to be saved from the wild thing that actually meant her no harm in hot pursuit. Then she was cornered - she had no where to run. She summoned up every ounce of confidence and mental strength she had, as she waved her shaking finger at him. Whilst telling him, 'how dare you do that to me'. Alfi pricked his ears, stared at her for a few seconds, then walked off. His job to help her find her courage that he knew was inside of her was complete.

Their relationship changed in those few seconds, they now instead share in a relationship of trust and mutual respect. He carries her on his back, no bridle or saddle in sight. They spend many happy hours together exploring our fields, as well as sunbathing together as she lies on his back.

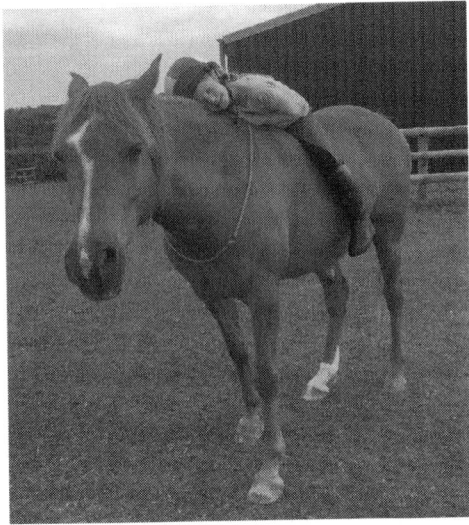

The Variable Compatibles

Any of the other personalities at any one time - this will be dependant on which personalities are dominant and how often the variables are shown.

The Free Thinking Truth Seeker

This type of personality may be viewed as a bit of a challenge by some trainers and owners. They will not bow down to the will of the trainer and in some cases, would rather be beaten to a pulp than summit to what they know is not truthful. That said, this does not mean that these horses will display outward aggression, more likely they will show a lack of compliance and acceptance of what it is you are asking of them, as they feel they are not being asked correctly. Some may choose to express their distaste of certain requests from others, or for the way in which the request is made. The manner in which the request is made, may in some cases, result in frustration for the horse causing them to 'act out'. These may come in the free expression of biting, kicking or other behaviours many humans may feel are undesirable. However, it should always be considered that such behaviour have a foundational cause. The owner or trainer that is able to identify such behaviour as information and frustration, rather than aggression, will always be of huge benefit to these horses. As well as, these horses being of huge benefit to them and their own education of horses and psychology.

The Free Thinking Truth Seeker Compatibles

All of the personalities; thought the dominant may be annoying for them at times. The personalities he can take under his wing and need extra care or are like minded will be his most compatible.

The Introvert

The introvert thrives best in smaller herds. His attention is quiet and thoughtful; he is a deep thinker. He is very sensitive to atmospheres and will do his best to avoid arguments, but if pushed too far he may be seen to stand his ground and then walk away. His way of both making his stand and disengaging from conflict.

He may be seen as a bit of a loner, preferring time alone or in smaller groups. He does not like to be pushed out into the foreground, instead preferring to hide behind others in his own quiet company. He should not be forced to engage, as to do so would mean stepping over his personal boundaries and therefore, invasively into his private mind space that is as important to him as his physical space.

Over the years he is unlikely to change; this is his natural way of being and it is innate to him, deep within him.

He will have his likes and dislikes, but no matter what is put before him (unless too much that it overrides him) he will always offer his best effort. Should his best effort be 'stamped on', or not acknowledged, it will lead to him close down and his insecurity will be fed. He will search for acknowledgment in what he offers. Not by way of flattering his ego, but rather, as an inner need to boost his confidence and thus drive him forwards. He is kind and earthy but in some cases he may possess a quick and fiery temper. The better he is listened to and adaption is made to work within in his mental boundaries (he has difficulty thinking outside of the box and craves routine) the safer he will feel. Do not spread his knowledge and teachings too thinly or expect him to enter into areas, both mental and physical that are over stimulating for him. This horse craves peace and security and his education broken down into bite sized chunks.

The Introvert Compatibles

The free thinking truth seeker, other introverts and sometimes the lost and lonely. The extrovert that complements his own traits and is compatible in the right way that helps to aid his confidence.

The Extrovert

This horse loves to be in a larger herd, the more that listen to what he has to say and offer, the better he will perform for his audience. He is a teacher of sorts and once his confidence is found it is used to his advantage. Many will learn from what he has to offer, so long as it is coming from the right place and he does not allow ego to override.

He is a double edged sword in as much as when his confidence is there it is there, but when it is waning he can retreat into his shell. Only to emerge renewed again when he feels that the time is right. He is more sensitive than he lets on. Some individuals may create the illusion of 'all is well', whilst deep inside they harbour a deep and unresolved past. Their 'now', enabling them to believe otherwise and a mask to wear, that allows them to hide their sorrows not just from others, but themselves at times as well.

There is not much more that I can say about the extrovert, as he is so deep and meaningful inwardly, that at times he will be hard to work out, due to the mask he wears. But his nature is one to be nurtured, as he is in, and will likely for some time be in a state of growth. Only hindered by the invasion of others, daily duties and should it befall him, ill health.

He is on a quest to find not only his inner self, but find a way in which the world and those in it reflect in such a way that they tie into a bigger picture for him. He is not the ego many would lead us to believe he is.

The Extrovert Compatibles

The complementary introvert, the free thinking truth seeker, he will be able to handle some dominant personalities that are strong, but only if they are strong in the right way.

The Stubborn

This personality is the tester of others, rigid in his mindset and to some degree unaware of the full complexity and needs of others. He is stuck to within his own mind and expects others to 'pussy foot' around him. In some individual cases others will be expected to 'bend to his will' most, if not all of the time.

His rigid mindset limits him in his ability to be the seeking free thinker. Why learn or do more when it suits him this way? Why put more effort in than he needs to? More often than not these horses will be heavier in body frame, rather than the lighter breeds, but this is not a hard and fast rule.

Most likely he will not put more effort into anything than is required (in his opinion) unless of course there is something in it for him. The more you push, the more frustration he causes, 'no skin of his nose' if you are pulling your hair out. He quite simply thinks you should learn the lesson he is offering (his one sided biased one) for which there is only one answer - his way or the highway.

In most cases he will have only a few close companions, if any. Only those of lower rank and that find comfort in his apparent and sometimes fake confidence tend to be drawn to him, others simply tolerate him. He will often be seen grazing alone, are we surprised at that?

His stereotype may predict that fast work is too much effort, why should he work harder than needed? Especially when he can stay in his own company and eat grass unhindered. He has the ability to test the patience of the saint and is the control freaks nightmare. This horse actually has a lot to offer others about themselves, if only in some cases how not to be. Amazing insights can be offered by them. Once we find out what is hidden beneath that mask they choose to wear.

The Stubborn Compatibles

The free thinking truth seeker

The Anxious

This type of horse personality will more often than not have a high head carriage. Or at least when his head carriage is low, the slightest unknown noise or sudden change will suddenly raise his head. His movements are quick and deliberate and may even appear clumsy at times. If suddenly something moves and startles him, he will be quick to react.

His anxiety may have been caused by his past; he may come from a history of abuse or neglect. It could even be the case that his neurotransmitters are misfiring, causing him to have issues with passing information and instruction through his brain, causing him confusion. Maybe he is just nervous in nature, maybe it is hereditary, it could be that he is not the only one that this way in his breeding line? It could be that he was not neglected or abused in the physical sense, but that he spent years with a novice owner. One who often aired their frustration, due to their own inability to instruct him and achieve a desired result - maybe that is what has caused him to be this way?

People will feel sorry for him as they see his muscles tense and see him stomach held in, as if poised ready to flee should he need too. His sudden movements will put some on edge. They will move, he will jump, they then jump because he does and the ongoing cycle of bouncing off of each other's anxiety continues. Wearing each other out and not aiding either party.

Maybe he is suffering from Post Traumatic Stress Disorder (PTSD). His trauma stuck within every cell of his body, as it has never found a way out and to release itself. It could be that the snowball effect has brought him to where he is now. The anxiety may have increased for him over time through being fed, even thought the original cause may have been minor. No one may have dealt with it back then, thus enabling a situation where it has been able to grow.

The Anxious Compatibles

The free thinking truth seeker, the introvert, the calmer of the institutionalised.

The Institutionalised

The personality that does what he is told without question, so long as it is within his physical capabilities. He doesn't know he is allowed to question; he just believes this is the way it is, 'follow thy master and his instruction'.

Each time he is reprimanded, he just accepts it as part of his life. Being shut in his stable for hours on end is normal to him - it is just how it 'is'. He maybe suffering from Post Incarceration Syndrome (PICS) that has created a state of learned helplessness in him, that he has been unable to shake off. If that has been his past till now, he may also be displaying anti- social personality traits towards other horses, have difficulty fitting into a herd, or forming a relationship with humans and other horses.

His prolonged solitary confinement, or prolonged years of silence due to not being allowed a voice, may have deprived him of sensory stimulation - other than having orders shouted at him.

It could be that people didn't realise they were being unkind, that they never meant him any harm, but that this has been the result for him none the less. His ability to play may be lacking, as he has only known work and the ability to play is not within him and nor does he know where to search inside of himself for that feeling of letting go in order to play. Maybe it just overwhelms him and he freezes?

Now he is allowed a voice, he is unable to find it. He may be scared to leave his stable and venture onto grass with other horses to relax and graze, as his feet have never known anything beneath him other than a sand school and filthy straw.

The Institutional Compatibles

The free thinking truth seeker, the introvert, (loneliness likes company) so in some cases the lost and lonely.

The Lost and Lonely

Maybe the saddest personality of all? He may not feel at home anywhere - his stable, his field, his herd or in a another's company. Though some of these things may feel acceptable to him, maybe even grow on him, making his life palatable. If he is lucky he will find the right person or horse that will understand him, so he has an ally in life and someone to turn to.

His ability to engage with others, both in relationships and in one off situations is impaired. He views the world as if looking through a gold fish bowl. He can see the world outside of him, he knows it is there and yet he does not feel in anyway part of it. He may as well not even be here....he thinks?

If he is lucky, in time he may be able to form a friendship with another horse that has singled him out and knows he needs help. Maybe this will be the truth seeker and free thinker of the herd that holds compassion and understanding for his situation. The one that is able to read him in a way the others can't.

If no such person or horse exists in his world, he will spend most of his time alone grazing away from the herd. Unless an inner desire to join the others is there and he knows 'how'. His inability to mix and blend in may not be there, he may try repeatedly to gain his place in the herd. Only to find himself an outcast as he just does not 'fit in'. He is different and the other herd members know this, he is not one of them and is of no benefit to them. In fact his incessant pestering of other herd members, due to his inability to properly engage may even be an annoyance to the herd and they may let him know this to his cost.

The Lost and Lonely Compatibles

The free thinking truth seeker, the introvert and in some cases the extrovert that offers himself as a confident leader - if he is of the correct attitude and traits.

The Dominant

This personality is two fold; the dominant that is insecure so enforces his 'will' on others, as a way of boosting his own confidence, and the dominant that is naturally dominant in nature that may also be caused by hormones or other factors.

The dominant personality expects others to bend to his will. He will likely (but not always) physically attack and bully to get his point across. At the very least he will be a face puller. He may be prone to tantrums, should he be in the company of one that will not bow down to him. In the male of this personality, mares will likely be 'his' property and other males may find themselves being chased off and excluded.

He may also display his dominance towards people. He can be a hard horse to get along with. Your best bet is to comply to avoid conflict when in his presence, if you are unable to play him at his own game. By tricking his mind in to thinking your idea was his all along. He is not one to be challenged, but rather, one to work along side. Let him think it was his idea, let him think he has won even when he has offered what you set out to achieve. Include him, do not isolate him, else his anger and dominance may soar.

The dominant in a wild herd and even in some cases the domesticated one, will have his place. He will keep in check any youngsters and wayward characters. To some degree if he is not an outright bully, he may aid in the smooth running of the herd, if he does not allow his ego to get the better of him or his hormones to override his role.

The Dominant Compatibles

In certain cases the free thinking truth seeker. If the dominant is not an outright bully - for the same reason also the introvert.

In certain cases the lost and lonely that are looking for strength, structure and guidance to lead them, if bullying is not part of the relationship and the dominance shows as strength.

THE MAYHEM

As we have already discussed in a previous chapter, not all personalities are compatible. These may be in the form of and include, inter horse-human relationships and inter horse-horse relationships.

One type of personality may cause anxiety and concern for the other party, when they exhibit traits that allow energy to rise in another in a non beneficial manner. This may be seen in the form of an anxious owner with an anxious horse. In such a relationship the highly distorted frequencies of their energy with bounce from one party to another, with no escape or chance of being transmuted by a calm and balanced individual. The anxiety may come through fear or the individual's past. Until such a time that it is dealt with, acknowledged and released, each party with suffer.

I saw a good example of this several years ago. A lady had bred a horse out of her calm mare. The (now gelded) youngster was an exceptionally sensitive soul and he would react suddenly to high energy, when he sensed it from others. Due to his quick and sudden reactions, his highly strung owner had become afraid of him. This created a situation that caused every meeting between them to be fretful for both parties. Due to this, his owner had done very little basic training with him on the ground, even though he was three and a half by the time I met him. This meant that every time something needed to be done, such as his teeth inspected by a dentist or his feet attended to by a Farrier, there would be 'behaviour'. I was present when he was seen for the first time by a dentist. I was not in a working capacity; I was just there as I knew the owner. Unfortunately the dentist that had been booked was not one I would have even considered to have chosen. Based on reputation and the fact he was not qualified either. My recommendation of a good qualified EDT that I knew and used had fallen on deaf ears.

Rather than befriend the young gelding, the dentist marched straight up to him and made eye contact, staring him straight in the face. No time was given for the young horse to sniff him, explore him and ease his feelings towards a new person entering into his space.

I am sad to say the result was that the horse reared and the dentist punished him by kicking him in the ribs. Am I surprised? - Sadly no, as I knew as soon as I met this man that he was not the sort that horses would feel comfortable around. His energy was harsh, arrogant and bolshy. The dentist went on to do the young gelding's mother's teeth - rather too quickly if you ask me. He then left and I hope he has never been booked to do their teeth since.

The sad thing about this experience is that horses learn by association. To this young boy now, having someone mess with your teeth can bring discomfort, physical harm and distrust. Not only were his teeth never checked, I am sure that when the next person tried, it would not have been a pleasant experience for either party, no matter how good the new dentist was. Due to the fact that the horse would be expecting pain that would then in turn, induce the feeling of fear. What a sad and worrying cycle.

Unfortunately for this young horse it was a

similar tale with the Farrier. His first experience was good, a Farrier that loved to play with young horses and did not care about being late for clients and had an interest in behaviour. His introduction to the horse was good. He walked him, turned him and rewarded him for lifting his feet and within forty minutes all four hooves were neatly trimmed without issue.

Sadly the Farrier's inability to stick to appointments, which caused him to turn up as much as six hours late, caused the owner to change Farrier. Whilst the new one was quiet, he did not really take the time to introduce himself to the horse. Instead wading in and just picking up the feet of this highly sensitive immature gelding and 'expecting' him to comply. Result being front legs over the top of a nearby five bar gate. Yet again another professional that had failed to see, meet with, and recognise the sensitivity of a beautiful young horse.

I must admit I had a soft spot for this lad. His high energy was not really him, just a manifestation of how certain individuals caused him to feel. He had been hit by his owner due to her own fears, in a bid to dominate and control him. Like that was ever going to work - but with me he was different. I would go into the field with him sometimes. We would just stand together quietly together. I would close my eyes, breath deeply and allow my heart rate to slow down. He would show me his signs of release, he would breathe out, yawn, lick and chew and flutter his eye lashes. Safe in the knowledge that beside him stood someone that never meant him any harm and enabled him to feel comfortable and bring his energy levels down. We would stand for five to fifteen minutes like this. He would then follow me around the field. He would stop and graze for a while, then lift his head and look at me as we repeated the process again, to enable him to know that this feeling - this peace could last.

One day his owner turned up only twenty minutes later. She put a head collar on him and led him up to the fence. She then told me excitedly that this was the first time she had been able to do so without him threatening to rear - I wonder why!

Sadly I witnessed many battles between this young horse and his owner. They were totally unsuited; each was scared of the other. I tried to explain to the owner one day, that every time he saw her walking across the field he was thinking 'oh dear, here comes the bollocking'. She just laughed and thought it funny. How can you truly help in a situation like that, other than offer comfort to the horse? As and when you can, so that they know 'someone' is there and not all humans are to be distrusted.

It was interesting to observe that the horses that he chose to be with were not his own herd, but instead my two Arabians. Two horses that were equally as sensitive as himself, horses that through their gentle and sensitive handling were quiet and low energy (other than when in play mode) That have a normal and low breath and heart rate due to their relaxation and peace of mind. No wonder he chose to spend so many hours by the fence, just to be in their presence. Just the act of doing this enabled his mind and body to relax and synchronise with theirs. This is a perfect example of how an inter horse-horse relationship can work well and how much it is needed.

From what I have heard he was up for sale for a while, then not for sale, kept, sent away and backed. I do wish him well and hope he is safe and happy as he is too beautiful to be destroyed, due to a lack of being understood for the beautiful sensitive being that he is.

The above story as you can see shows only too clearly, how different personalities and energies can affect each other. Not only this, but how anxiety can be created through the mixing of those energies, without daily physical punishment needing to be present. A horse that is unable to relax is a horse that feels insecure and unsafe. The longer that these feelings go on, the more it enables the horse's mind and body to become stuck in this cycle of anxiety that he has no control over. Although his anxiety may start out as on and off, dependent on who the horse is with and his experiences and encounters. If there is no let up and this continues over a period of time without any form of release in between, the horse will become 'stuck' mentally. Not only will he have an increased heart rate and breathing pattern (including holding his breath), but he will also release adrenalin and cortisol. Neither of which will be beneficial to his physical body. In fact scientific studies have shown that excessive and prolonged cortisol release can in some cases, result in varying degrees of brain damage.

Do we really want to destroy our horses mentally, emotionally and physically - breaking their inner spirit? If not, then we have to act, not just for their sake, but also for our own to enable us to relax and not worry also.

I think that a lot of readers will be able to identify with at least one area of concern within the relationship, or requests we offer to our horse. Whether that be leading, trailer loading, not being able to stop them in fast work or having difficulty being able to keep their focus. If you are not experiencing any of these issues currently, then it is likely that in the past you will have, or that you have come across them with other horses.

I also feel at this point it is extremely important to recognise the difference between punishment and correction. Punishment is information that we give the horse that is mentally or physically negative and even threatening. When this act is carried out it comes from a place of dominance, anger, fear or frustration. It is the information that states 'this is not what I asked for, you have done it wrong' (often accompanied by aggression). Sadly this is where it tends to end for the horse information wise. The horse is left worried, confused and often anxious and not really understanding what it is that you actually do want.

Correction is totally the opposite end of this scale information wise. Correction is the information we give the horse that tells him, 'this is not what I am looking for – so try this' and it comes in the form of positive reinforcement. To better explain this I will give you an example of it.

For whatever reason the horse has reared - in this scenario we will first look at punishment. As the horse rears the handler faces the horse (predator confrontation mode) and he pulls on the lead rope to try and bring the horse's front end back down to the ground. This is exceptionally dangerous in itself, as this will cause most horses to pull back, which may result in them going over on their back or falling sideways. I have sadly also seen horses land only to have their lead ropes given a sharp tug, jolting down hard on their sensitive poll area as punishment.

What information does this give to the horse?

Other than you were wrong to come down and stand beside me?

If you are handling a horse that is likely to rear, please make sure you are wearing safety gear including gloves. Clip a long lead rope to the head collar or halter. Breathe out a few times and wait for the horse to relax, before you ask *anything* of him. Reward him quietly for any positive signs of release that he offers.

Should the worst happen and he does rear, stand back, let the rope out, stand sideways to him so that no eye contact is made but you can still see what he is doing and *ignore him.* Yes that's right, *ignore him!* Once he has come down he has given you what you were looking for. By not punishing him you have not escalated his fear or frustration and you have enabled him to come down more quietly. Now breathe deeply and stand beside him. Continue to breathe, wait a few seconds and then *reward him - yes reward him.* You are not rewarding him for rearing, that part of this episode is now over. Rather, by pausing once he is down and stood quietly with you and rewarding him. You are in fact telling him, 'yes, this is the response I am looking for from you'.

With the reward in place and reinforced in the horses mind, that rearing did not in fact get him anywhere. He has now learnt that it is far more rewarding and comfortable to instead stand quietly. Now wait until he is calm a little longer, not forgetting to periodically reward him for his positive behaviour. Watch for a slowing of his breathing and his signs of release. Once you have seen these positive changes, reward him and then ask him to lead quietly again.

By responding to him in this way he will learn that his negative expression of energy was not needed. That it was stressful and of no benefit to him, whilst keeping calm is.

Now Let Us Consider:

Why did he feel the need to rear?

What were we doing at that moment?

Were we thinking of something else?

Was our body rigid?

Were we upset?

Were we ignoring him?

Were we asking him to do something that scared him, or that he did not understand?

Were we missing the signs he was offering that said, 'this is too much for me'?

Whatever his reason for rearing is, it will have been valid to him at the time. Just a simple change in our response to him, what we ask of him and how we ask it, can result in a very different and much safer outcome.

If we hit him for his behaviour, shout at him, or react to him with fear or some other negative response, all we do is cause further distress. The psychology of the rear is, 'I can not see how I can go forwards' or 'evasion'. It is not the horse refusing and going against your request, he is simply telling you he is at that moment in time unable to respond to it in the way you are looking for. In fact, he may not even understand what you are asking him at all. Therefore how indeed can he respond as expected?

Unfortunately there is a bit of ego in the horse world in general, thankfully not completely. Some choose to seek out horses that are too big, too strong and not at all physically or mentally matched to themselves, in a bid to impress others. Thereby over horsing themselves and causing both themselves and their horse anxiety and misery. This is an all too common story that has seen the euthanisation of many horses, as well as beatings, injuries and mental collapse. As well as many injured and anxious riders and owners that have struggled on, in a bid not to admit that they have made a bad decision for both parties.

Neither the horse, nor the owner will benefit from a partnership such as this, or rather the lack of partnership in the long term. The idea of horse ownership is that we are meant to enjoy each others company and working life, if we have one. It does not matter what our horse looks like, how big they are or what colour they are. It is the relationship, trust and comfort of each party that is important, no matter what that partnership may entail. Whether you are a competition rider or a happy hacker, or even if you do not ride at all. It is important that there is consistency, kindness, respect and consideration and the all important acknowledgment between you. When all of these elements are in place there is no need for us, or any desire felt, to step over the boundaries into a place of disrespect for the horse.

Another way that mayhem may manifest itself is through the inability to understand the difference between sympathy and empathy, and how they impact upon our horses so differently, dependent on which we feel. In simple terms sympathy is weakness and the allowance of being dragged into another's drama. This causes us to make their emotional baggage our own; causes stress and causes worry. Empathy on the other hand, is the ability to see and feel from another's perspective, without it overly having an effect on our own emotional state. It is not that we do not care, that we do not love them and do not have concern for them. It is simply that we understand that this is their drama and that the best way we can support them, is to recognise it as such. By being able to step back in such a way, it enables us to see things more logically, rather than allowing negative emotions to override. It is all very well feeling sorry for our horse if they have come to us from a bad past. But what they need is for us to help them start that new life and be strong for them. If we are unable to do this and instead choose a path of sympathy, we can not help but have a negative affect on them. We grow anxious and upset ourselves and then reflect those feelings onto our horses, which can cause their own emotional state to overflow.

Empathy is always key to a good relationship, due to it enabling us to stand back without worry and keep calm. The calmness your horse needs when they feel under pressure. Let them have their drama, do not engage in it or escalate it with misplaced emotions of sympathy. Just be there for them and support them by creating a quiet and calm environment.

Sadly sympathy is often the reason why so many horses lack boundaries and over step them so easily. The reason being is that the owners do not stick to and implement the boundaries themselves. What we tell our horse is not acceptable one day, we may tell them is the next. If they have been able to do it this time, the next time they repeat it and are corrected for it. They will not only be confused, they will also loose trust in us due to our lack of consistency. The biggest cause of our inconsistent behaviour is often feeling sorry for our horse and/or our own lack of focus and observation of their needs. When we feel sorry for them we often forget that boundaries and keeping them in place, is in fact, what helps our horses feel secure and build in confidence. The greatest kindness we can offer a troubled horse is empathy over sympathy. As the outcome of this will be our offering of calmness, relaxation and a safe company in which to heal and work through their issues. Where sympathy reins there will always be the potential for issues to arise, but where empathy reins, we will be better mentally equip to help them.

I am privileged enough to have three beautiful Arabian horses in my care at this present time. Each one of them has his own unique personality, likes and dislikes and outward behaviours. None of my horses live up to the often unfair stereotype vision of the flighty and highly strung Arab. Arabians are sensitive, intelligent and often one person type personalities. I put their outward demeanour very much down to their handling and life style. They live together as a small herd and have freedom all of the time. The yard gate is left open, enabling them to go into their shelter and open stables anytime they like, where they will also find their slow hay feeders in bad weather. There are no arguments, no fallings out or squabbling. They live peacefully, safe in the freedom of mind that their life will be as easy as I can make it for them. I value each of my horses in their own right and respect them for the unique characteristics and personality traits that each has.

We are often guilty of wanting to shape our horses into the mould we desire. Choosing a breed best suited to dressage, jumping or endurance without considering the individual's personality. We may even look at their bloodlines to see what the dam and sire of our horse were good at. We may even have bought our horse due to this, as it is the same discipline for which we intend for our purchase. No matter what a horse's bloodline, physical make up or past working life, it is by no means a hard and fast rule that this is the work best suited to 'our' horse mentally. Fair enough he may perform well, he may not refuse, but is he happy doing what is expected of him?

Rather than just look to the physical body, we also need to access the personality make up of our horse and what they are best suited to as a whole. It is no point having a horse that does not want to jump if that is our primary intent. To force a horse to jump when his heart is not in it will breed contempt, refusal and maybe even behaviour issues. Being of the correct physical make up is just not enough; personality and interest are just as important. Not only must we be well matched mentally and physically with our horse, we must also be compatible work wise.

'Get him a stronger bit, kick him on, give him a smack and get him out of your face'.

All of these sayings have stuck with me since I have heard them. Never once did the people using them think, or even consider that the horse in question had a justified reason for their behaviour. How horses must wish they had voices like our own, to enable them to scream at us when we hurt them? When the cold hard metal is pulled and pressed on their sensitive flesh, nerves and bone and when the hard leather stick hits them. Maybe if they had a voice that enabled them to scream and us to truly 'hear' what kind of mayhem and distress we are causing them – then, maybe it would be different. So is it right that they suffer through their vocal chords being different from our own?

Stronger bits do not help; whips do not help. All they do is cause pain and distress and close down the horse due to this - the horse that dare not scream at you physically through fear of further punishment and pain. It is only when we remove all of these things, stand with our horse and ask him *'show me who you really are'*, that he is able to be himself in a way we can recognise as we are willing to *'see'* him. This is the new foundation to building him up into the horse that he is, instead of the one we desire him to be.

Gone are the days that I will attend a horse show as a spectator. The displays of handlers and riders fighting angry or scared horses and whipping them when they do not comply are over for me. This is something I have no wish to witness. Displays of this nature, the handling and the aggressive riding I have often seen there, have no space in the life of a horse. They deserve better and are better than that. For each horse I have observed in this situation, I could write a list of reasons for their behaviour due to the handling and riding I have witnessed. I hope one day the showing world will change and that such disgusting displays of behaviour from people is condemned, instead of being rewarded in the form of coloured ribbons. Until such a time mayhem will continue and flourish at great cost to our horses. As humans we need to wake up and start to look more deeply into the psyche of the horse and learn to question.

What is it that we are doing to them that is creating such anguish for them?

How we can help them?

How we can live in harmony with no need to fight?

THE LIVE DEMONSTRATION

Over the years I have attended many live horse related demonstrations. One thing that has become obviously apparent is, the lack of focus between instructor and horse. In a live demo situation there will be an audience that the instructor will need to engage with. As they work the horse they explain to the audience what they are doing and why, maybe even explaining the horses response - this is where the issue lies.

The moment the instructor takes his focus from the horse to focus on the audience. Connection between instructor and horse to a large degree has been lost. Whilst the instructor may still be observing the horse's body language and responding with his own; his mind is elsewhere and not fully with the horse.

When this disconnection is made the horse is out on a limb, whilst the physical actions may still remain, the energetic focus and intent is sadly lacking. The horse is only receiving part of the information he needs. During these lapses of connection between horse and instructor, the horse may slow of even stop his response. This is only natural as full communication is not being achieved.

Once the instructor has explained to the audience, he now brings his intention and focus back to the horse. If the horse has slowed due to lack of instructor input, in order to rebuild the momentum, the instructor must then reinforce their request and likely will do so will more force. The finesse and subtlety has flown right out the window.

Let us view this for a moment from the horse's perspective. Instruction is given (hopefully correctly) so he willingly responds. He understands what is being asked of him and how to respond which hopefully he does, if there are no underlying issues. He is now having a conversation with the instructor. Suddenly and without warning the instructor, the person he is engaged with, allows his mind to wander and instead creates a link with the audience. The instructor is now talking at the audience, not to him. Add to this the lack of contact and confused signals as the instructor is largely focused elsewhere and it is only too obvious why the horse alters his response. (Or if feeling unsettled he may even continue to do what he is doing, but wonder why he is doing it, so continues, due to a lack of knowing what else to do).

Now let us put this into context. Some one speaks to us; we respond and a connection and conversation is created. That person then turns to someone else and creates a connection with them. Whilst they are doing this, they likely answer 'yes I know what you mean' by way of a response to your input. You know they are not listening - you stop talking. They then finish their other conversation and bring their focus back to you, re-establishing a conversation. The momentum of that conversation picks up. After this has happened a few times you are starting to feel a little ignored. Are they actually interested in engaging with you or not? You may loose interest or may become confused as to what is expected of you and how you should respond.

The only real difference here is that the instructor is to a large degree the initiator of the conversation. He is conducting a live demonstration and he must keep that going. In order to re-establish his connection with the now likely distracted horse, he must shout a little louder in order to regain his focus. This sadly then creates the scene for the minutes or hours to come until such a time as the demonstration ends. The horse is mentally exhausted.

I can still recall a live demonstration that I did some years ago. It was a healing demonstration, rather than a training one, but the classic issues still remain the same. When offering a healing session to a horse I do not tie them up. It is important to me and even more so them, that they are able to move away and out of my energy. This is in order that they can connect to and identify with the changes that have been created in their own energy.

I was in a round-pen with a little pony. The audience were gathered all around the sides observing. I made my connection with the pony and made to him my offering of the healing, that I hoped he would be willing to accept. Luckily he engaged in a connection with me and the conversation and healing between us was established. Then I made my connection with the audience to explain what I was doing, why and the response the pony was displaying. He then walked off.

The moment I had removed my focus from him, I had broken the conversational link that had been between us. He thought I was not interested and went to find someone that was. Only to be greeted by hands and smiles offered to him by the audience. To cut a long story short, the rest of the demonstration was given verbally, as I tried to mend my now broken demonstration and explain my reasoning.

There is a reason why I have re-laid the above story and that is because of the valuable lesson within it. This being, had I tied this little pony up so that he had to stay with me and comply. I would have been forcing my will onto him for the benefit of creating a good demonstration for an audience. That little pony who was my primary concern and should have been my primary focus, would have been 'used' for my own means of 'display', rather than it being a pleasurable and comfortable experience for him. He would have had to tolerate my inconsistent focus bouncing between him and the audience, whilst people may have liked the demonstration. It would have served no positive purpose for him at all and the purpose of the demonstration was to show people how to do it the best way for the pony.

So whilst to the casual onlooker it may have appeared that my demonstration had gone to pot. It had in fact taught a valuable lesson to those that understood what had been playing out. Those same people that have the pony's best interests at heart.

Since this time I have either just talked about the subject to an audience, or I have first explained to them in a demonstration what I am setting out to achieve. Why and how the horse is expected to respond, in light of what I am putting on offer for them. After the demonstration has then finished I discuss with audience the horse's responses, my responses and the conversation that has just been experienced between us. Not only does this help with my own concentration, but it makes it much nicer for the horse involved. As they know they have and can experience my full focus and engagement with them. I am listening with eyes, ears, heart and mind, rather than just going through the physical processes that so many instructors do.

In order to help the reader to understand a little more from the horses' perspective and how this breakdown in communication and focus creates issues for them, I have below, offered some further insights as to what I have witnessed whilst observing other live demonstrations.

Scene 1

Much of the demonstration has already taken place in the indoor school and it is nearing its end; the grand finale. Gone from the school are the three horses that were working together with their instructors. The same horses whose reactions were calm yet robotic, they have done it a hundred times before -they know what comes next, they know what is expected of them. So it doesn't matter if the focus from the instructor was not there in its entirety, they knew what came next and what response was expected of them. Their body's are so used to this routine that they respond without much thought. There were no hidden surprises for them. Their expressions were more of boredom and automatic response than interest.

Now a horse, complete with his rider on board and wearing a rope halter is in trot and approaching his first jump. The rider sits balanced, the horse clears the jump beautifully and proceeds to the next which he approaches and clears in much the same way. Now horse and rider are approaching their third jump, the horse lifts off in what appears to be a focused and balanced manner. The rider then turns his head to the audience, lifts his cowboy hat off his head and smiles at the audience expecting applause. The horse that is in mid flow looses his balance as the rider's weight shifts in the saddle, as he turns to impress his audience. The horse lands awkwardly and the silly man looses his hat, as he chooses to try and impress his audience, rather than focus on his steed. His disconnected focus and lack of communication with the horse, as well as taking away the fluidity of the horse's natural balance has caused them to stumble. The demonstration has not gone as he would have liked, I hope he learnt his lesson and understood why it happened.

Scene 2

It is evening and the sky is dark, I make my way into the indoor school where the demonstration is to take place. I make my way to a seat where I am sat up high and I can clearly see the round-pen. The horse is brought in, a lovely stallion of five years old that we are told has not yet been backed. Apparently this is the reason that he is here - to begin his ridden education. The lights are bright; the predators stare. The horse is feeling over stimulated and is being bombarded through his visual, audial and olfactory senses. Not to mentioned the heightened energy that exists in the atmosphere and is also feeding his fear.

The instructor uses his body language to start this young moving off around the round-pen. The horse seems agitated and unsure. He is not used to the fencing of the round-pen. Complete with hundreds of predators sat the other side staring at him. 'Who is this person issuing instructions?' He wonders.

He starts moving forwards at a steady pace without question. This is reinforced by the body language of the one speaking to him. Then the connection stops - this man, the one he is listening too that is meant to be offering instruction for him to follow and trying to create security and gain his focus in such a worrying and alien environment has stopped 'speaking'. Instead, his focus is now on the predators. The young stallion starts to slow, his head drops slightly and his eyes soften. The pressure is off and he is starting to feel slightly safer - then the connection is back. His head comes up, his eyes widen and he picks up his pace that is those moments of disconnection had started to waver, he is on the move again. The 'yo-yo' focus and disconnection of the instructor continues for some minutes, as the horse is forced to change direction through the cues being given that are being backed up with mental pressure. By now this Horse Whisper is shouting. The atmosphere, concern the horse is experiencing, along with vulnerability is all being felt by the horse. The Whisper is shouting to make him self heard, the shouting comes from his body, not his mouth. His only verbal connection is with the audience, not with the horse. The Whisperer's energy is being split between the two, as he tries to juggle connection with both but is failing. Hence the shouting continues to make sure the horse can hear him and keeps moving.

The young stallion grows weary, he has run hard. He surrenders to the man that has been shouting at him and he asks to be allowed come in as shown by his submissive behaviour. He can not keep running forever around this round-pen and the instructor knows this, just as well as much as he does - the instructor wins.

The young stallion has sought comfort in the presence of the Whisperer, rather than the on-going circles. The comfort offered by the lesser of two evils that would only bring comfort to the vulnerable. Comfort is found in that which is known and understood even when it is unkind.

Next someone else enters the round-pen. They are carrying a saddle and a bridle. These pieces of equipment are put on the horse. He has seen them before so gives them little attention as his focus is split between Whisperer, his aid, the pressurising atmosphere and the predators.

Something is strapped to his back. It is heavy and is meant to represent the weight of the rider. Oh dear - the Whisperer is now sending out the cues to get moving. He takes the hint and off around the round-pen he goes. It appears his comfort was only to be short lived.

Minutes pass as he keeps moving and the focus and connection of the Whisperer, once more flits between this young stallion and the predators. Once more the horse is invited in. The weight is removed from his back and replaced with the Whisperer's aid. He leans with his weight forward and asks the young stallion to move forwards with him. After a few minutes the horse relaxes - but only slightly. The man takes up the reins and applies pressure to the horse's delicate mouth by way of the bit and he backs up. The man dismounts and the crowd applauds. Apparently this horse's introduction to ridden work is complete. The crowd clap as I look around the school and see the smiling faces. I wonder why they are unable to see what I can. I put my head in my hands. I want to leave but my place in the seated crowd makes it difficult to do so. I have to sit and continue to watch the performance as the next horse is brought into the round-pen. I am wishing I could leave and not have to witness what is to come next.

Three months later my phone rang. It was a lady that had been having problems with her young stallion since he had been in a live demonstration. Our conversation brought about the realisation that this was the very same young horse I had witnessed in the round-pen months earlier. Am I surprised? Sadly - 'No'.

My Story

Today was the day that it felt 'right' for Alfi my chestnut Arabian to begin his ridden education. He was almost four and a half years old and had been with me since he was eleven months. Our work up until now had just involved ground work at liberty. He did not know the purpose of, or have the experience of running and moving in circles. As this was not something that had ever been part of his education or was innate to him. We spent a few minutes walking in the field together, as I asked him to 'walk on' and 'whoa' along side me. We stood in the field at liberty as I put on his head collar and his saddle. The same saddle he had only worn once before for a short in hand walk up the road, several weeks prior. He stood totally still as I gently lowered the saddle onto his back. He breathed out, his cue he felt safe so I waited a few seconds and then I started to tighten his girth. Still Alfi did not move, as little by little I secured it. He had the choice to move away, no pressure would be applied if he did - he chose to stay.

We walked to the fence together and he quietly lined up along side it. I breathed out - so did he. Quietly, I lifted my leg and allowed it to touch his back. His eyes widened - but just slightly, as he tensed his near fore. He was 'thinking' about moving so I removed my leg. I breathed out - again he followed my cue and relaxed. I waited a few minutes and then I touched his back with my leg again. This time he showed no sign of tension and within seconds I was on his back and we were walking quietly around the field. His ears back listening as we moved together. Two days later we repeated this process, only this time there was no tensing within his body as I mounted. We went for an amble up the road for ten minutes with my husband leading him. I could feel his confidence beneath me as he strode out. Then he put his head into the middle of my husband's back and shoved him into the grass verge. This horse did not need someone to hold his hand, he felt secure as his early training had set him up to seek, explore and bring to the surface his own internal confidence.

Scene 3

It was afternoon and so there was no artificial lightening in the indoor school. I went in and took my seat outside of the round-pen. The chairs were very close to the fencing of the round-pen - too close. A man entered with a horse and I watched the demonstration in horror. What I witnessed was pure unadulterated dominance.

The minutes ticked by as the horse was running around the round-pen. His eyes wide with fear, as a white plastic chair was thrown behind him. His backend tensed and his speed picked up. Next this man, this so called Horse Whisperer that was screaming at the horse, held in his hand a plastic bottle. He began to shake it hard and it made the most loud, annoying noise. It was now the turn of the loud plastic bottle to be thrown behind the horse, causing his pace moving up yet another gear.

The horse was (much to his relief) finally invited in. The trauma for a few minutes had come to an end. The horse stood quietly with the man as the man described the horse's background and how in the past this horse has badly injured him (can we blame him?). The man ground tied the horse and stood facing him as he just stared at the horse - the horse stood still. Suddenly the man leapt forwards and yanked down hard on the horses lead rope, causing pain over his poll and his head to flick. The man stood still again, as did the horse. I was finding this so hard to witness. I had to ask this man, 'why? 'why have you done this to this horse?'. With that I took a deep breath and stood up in front of everyone and asked him.

His reply was short and to the point 'because the last time this horse looked at me like that I ended up in hospital'. I think I must have been missing the point - in what way had this horse just looked at him? There was no anger or intent to injure in his eyes that I could see, he had not moved or tensed until such a time the pain shot through his poll.

I was dying to ask this man that screamed at horses in every way other than with words. If he thought it OK to punch in the face every person that looked at him in a way he was misinterpreted. I bit my tongue and headed to the door and left instead, what was the point? This was and remains to be the worst display of so called horse training that I have ever witnessed in the flesh.

Scene 4

It is a sunny afternoon and I enter the indoor school. People are milling around talking about horses, but this time something is different. The only thing I am able to put it down to is the difference in atmosphere. There is no tension, people are smiling and it feels comfortable to be here.

In front of us is a sand school so we take our seats at one end. There isn't any high fencing between us and the horse and we are all sat at one end of the building.

A man steps in, he is softly spoken, his body is relaxed and he talks to us with genuine passion about horses. This demonstration is different; this man that whispers to horses is not here to train horses. Rather, he sees his role today as educating riders to work with their own horse under his guidance. Thus enabling both horse and rider to have a comfortable and pleasant experience and seek knowledge, that they can then take home and continue with.

At one point a rider follows his instruction, the horse carries out the request right on cue, but not quite as well as expected. The Whisperer pauses, he looks deep in thought and then says 'hmmm I think I could have done that a better way'. This man and his passion for horses is growing on me.

For the next two hours I watch closely, as the people continue to work with their horse's. We have to watch closely for both the cue given by the rider and response offered by the horse, because this man seems to forgotten his audience. His focus is clearly on horse and rider, as indeed it should be.

I do not feel the need to say more, as I feel the words in my last story explain well enough the pleasure of that day when I saw this man, his work and how he was helping to make the life of horses better. Through educating their people rather than seeking to impress an audience.

The best way in which we can help a horse relax as a spectator, is to be aware of our own energy. All we have to do is relax and hold a soft aura about us – no rigidness. Try not to stare straight at the horse with unblinking eyes, as he will recognise this as predator hunting mode. Instead, soften your facial expression, do not make direct eye contact and remember to blink. As simple as this all sounds, the more spectators that do this, the more relaxed the horse is able to feel in his demonstration surroundings. Let's make it more comfortable for him.

THE MAGIC

An open mind and the ability to recognise our horses for what they truly are and how they can feel is without a doubt - the first step in enabling a harmonious relationship. When we allow preconceived ideas and doubt to fall away, we leave the door wide open for the magic to manifest.

The Centaur Experience is the term I give to the creation of this magic. When working side by side, it allows for the blending of the energies of both horse and owner (rider) to work as one, as well as the added connection of ideas and mutual understandings. During these times, valuable insights are offered by the horse and may come to us as if they were our own thoughts and ideas.

Being able to identify with our horse is fundamental in us being able to glimpse inside of his mind. Giving him the full acknowledgment and regard that he has worked so hard to create and earn. It is only through the closing of our minds, as well as our hearts, that the magic is unable to flow freely and without judgment in either side.

Consideration of how the horse feels in him-self will often be the acknowledgment sought and needed by our equine companions. When we are able to empathise with our humble friend the horse, the way in which we feel about them, think about them and consider them will all change. They will be able to notice the change in us, the softening of our energy and they will feel safe in our presence.

Certain horses will resonate with our own energies, like tuning forks that vibrate when in the same company of those that carry the same energy. Due to this, it may be that an owner that has been abused in the past is drawn to horses that have been abused in much the same way as they have been. It maybe that they are drawn to unconfident horses, as that is indeed how they themselves feel.

The key to the magical union is to take those horses that truly resonate with us into our care, no matter what their breed, age or physical form. These are the horses we can learn with, heal with and best live out our lives with. The horses that make our hearts sing and sometimes our hearts break, due to the feelings that they stir within us. What is in a relationship with our horse if it is missing the vital elements of love, joy, connection, empathy and our all valuable learning experiences in life?

They may teach us to ride, they may let us use their body's to sit and travel on, but what is in a ride if it is empty, not connected and purely physical?

So often I hear the all too familiar story of a person that set out to look for a certain breed or gender of horse, only to return home with something entirely different. Maybe even knowing from the first moment they saw the photograph of the horse on a computer screen advert, that this was the horse that was destined to be theirs. They may not have been able to rationalise it, give a reason - they just 'knew'.

In 2003 I went looking for my perfect horse. He was to be a yearling, a gelding, purebred Arabian, chestnut with a blaze and a flaxen mane and tail. Most importantly after my years and sorrows of taking care of sick and abused equines, he was to have nothing wrong with him. I needed a horse that would not cause concern, heartbreak or break the bank.

The first one that I found was born with a severally undershot lower jaw. He was cow hocked, run down, had a hunters bump that indicated lumber and sacral issues and was far from the ideal horse I was thinking of - and yet...I am a strong believer in fate - I went to see him anyway. Twelve years later he is still with me, we have a bond that I could not describe to others unless they have experienced it with their own horse. I describe it as the 'it thing'. You can't smell it, physically touch it or hear it, you can only feel it and when you have it, you just know, there is no describing it other than as an inner feeling that is undeniable.

Over the years he has suffered from several serious illnesses. He has almost died and he is no longer ridden, due to his lumber and sacral issues catching up with him. After he has been sat down for a while and gets up, he needs to stand for a few minutes as his leg will have gone numb. He sometimes bites when you are not listening fully or understanding him fast enough; he is opinionated and stubborn. He is not a fan of ridden work, even if his health held that option open to him. Yet he has the biggest most truthful heart of any horse that I have ever met.

Maybe this is why we get on so well and respect and understand each other? In the morning when I get out of bed I am sore. My sacrum presses on nerves that slows my legs down and makes my muscles in my back, pelvis, neck and shoulders sore. I can get up off a chair and have to sit down again as I feel my back start to give way. I am opinionated, stubborn and a truth seeker; just like Alfi. I have long standing chronic illnesses that have driven my immune system down. I have no desire to ride a horse anymore even if I could manage to get on and off safely. Yet like Alfi,I do not give up as I have a heart felt desire to make a difference for both horses and humans and how they view the world of interspecies relationships. I understand Alfi and I understand that physical health, or lack of it does not have to hold either of us back.

Several years ago when Alfi and I were still riding together, a thought came to mind and through that, was born my idea of the Centaur Experience and what this little chestnut Arabian was trying to teach me. This was not about me being the rider and he my horse that was under my instruction. This was about us becoming as one and creating that sacred connection through heart, mind and energy. I knew what I needed to do; but I was scared. I was scared that I would fail and that in failing, I would let him down.

Soon after this, I was running a workshop with another Therapist. One of the ladies on the workshop was an Equine Physiotherapist and had brought her husband along with her, who was a competition rider. Half way through the day the co-facilitator of the workshop turned to me and in front of everyone, told me that 'now was the time'. I needed to go outside and ride Alfi in the way that he was asking for. I immediately burst in to tears and felt stupid, as everyone starred wondering what an earth was wrong with me. How could I make them understand how scared I was? What if I let my horse down? I could have backed out if I wanted to - a simple 'no' would have been enough. But then I would never know what it was like to feel that way - maybe I should try?

I went out into the field with the gentleman that was a competition rider. I climbed onto my horse bareback and just sat there. I closed my eyes, I took a deep breath and then everything changed. It was as if I had become him and yet at the same time, I was aware that I was still myself. The rest fell into place automatically as I brought energy up through my arm as if it were his off fore leg and he suddenly, but deliberately moved forward on that same leg. He then came to a standstill the moment I thought that too. We did it together again with the other leg. I then dismounted and stood with my horse and cried and thanked him in the full knowledge that it didn't matter if we never did it again, as we knew we could.

You see, this was not just about being able to ride with my energy and thought in this way. This was about my fears and how my horse was helping me to heal and release those fears. By placing his trust in me and coaching me gently in a way he knew he could support me.

What human would have known how to do this?

Known how to go about it?

Or even have recognised this fear in me?

Who could have?

Other than the one that feels just like me and knows me as if I were him.

I have no doubt that some readers will wonder what all the fuss is about. Why it was such a big deal to me and why and how this changed my life. All I can tell you is that it was one of the most profound events of my life. In that moment magic was created; the wall between the horse and human world's collapsed and the divide disappeared. In that moment I became horse and my horse became human, enabling us both to experience that unity of horse and human, the Centaur in every sense of the word.

After this I only rode Alfi a few more times before we decided it was time to give up riding for both our sakes, due to our physical structural issues. It is no longer needed or part of our relationship. We know we can if we need to, but we have no use for it. Our relationship now exists on the ground, where we can look each other in the eye and observe the energies and facial expressions more clearly. Where we can run, play and communicate in comfort and freedom.

I found my perfect horse that day, the sickly little youngster that sent me on an search for natural medicine and therapies to help him to heal. The information for which has been two fold, as it has had a dramatic affect in my work as an Equine Therapist and Communicator. It has enabled me to help and advise other owner's as to how they too can help their horses. As well as, enabling me to hear from the horses themselves first hand, what it is that they need. Not a day has gone by since, that has not caused me to question, ponder, research and think. That day out in the field changed me; change can be scary and it can create fear. Unless we take the bit between our teeth and run with it, we will never know just how life changing those positive experiences can be. They allow us to step out of our rigid way of thinking, enabling us to find our confidence and 'know', deep down in our hearts what is truth, right or just plain fantasy or lie.

Only a few weeks after I had backed Alfi I was sat watching the evening news. It showed floods in the Netherlands that had stranded a hundred horses and foals on what was by now an island. They were all huddled together. Some sadly had already fallen into the water and drowned. Efforts to send boats out to lead the horses back to dry land had failed, due to causing fear within the large concerned herd.

Things were set to look worse for the horses, until several ladies arrived on their horses. These brave ladies swam out on horseback on their equally as brave steeds and led the herd through the water to safety. I watched in awe as the event unfolded as I watched. Then loud and clear I heard a voice that said. 'I would have done that for you if you asked me too'. I burst into tears as the goose bumps shot up my arms and legs, as my nervous system acknowledged the truth behind Alfi's words. Yes, if I had asked this horse that gives me his all, his trust and companionship. He would have done it for me without question - that I have never doubted and never will. It was a knowing of truth that I felt in that moment right to my very core.

Horses can help us to heal our fears, maybe even bringing to light those that are buried so deeply within our subconscious. Even those that at first we do not even recognise the existence of, until the day that our horse supports us in a way that they can be felt and brought to light. Allowing ourselves to feel vulnerable is not weakness, the weakness is in our denial of vulnerability and our unwillingness to work through it and face it. Instead we choose to mask it with a persona that has no authentic foundation.

Horses see right through our fake persona; they see past the lies we tell, even to ourselves. They know who we are the moment we walk into the field. The moment we open ourselves to them and lay ourselves bare to them, they know our strengths and our fears and they know what it is we need to learn and experience. They know the challenges we need to face and so often offer them to us with an open heart. Once we conquer our fears with their help and support, life changes and we may never have to experience those lessons and fears again. Should we choose to acknowledge and accept it the first time it is presented - rather than denying the offering given to us by our horse.

The horses ask you to keep an open mind, keep questioning their reasoning. Even if the answers do not come easily at first, you will find them. Horses are so much more than their physical body's, they are more than blood, flesh and bone with chemicals thrown into the mix. They are living, breathing, sentient beings - living entities with a life path, loves, fears and journeys of their own. They stumble upon our paths as our teachers, our healers, our wise councils and our friends. They allow us to cry into their manes and they share in our joy, our sorrows, fears and achievements.

None of us are perfect; our horses are learning also. For many of us the lesson is that of tolerance without emotional collapse, self esteem without ego and fortitude in the face of adversity. Let us be both his student and his teacher and let him be ours.

RESOURCES

Holly Davis
Animal Communicator and Therapist
Natural Medicine and Behaviour
www.hollydavis.co.uk

Sue Gardner
Senior Instructor – Applied Behaviour
www.appliedbehaviour.co.uk
Horse Agility Associate Instructor
www.horsebehaviourandtraining.co.uk
www.horseagilityclub.com

Elenore Bowden-Bird
Aulanda Park Liberty
www.apequineliberty.com.au

Graeme Green
Horse Healing and Land Healing
www.themindfulhorse.wordpress.com

Susan Duckworth
Hoofboots, Bitless Bridles, Neem and much
more.
www.bitlessandbarefoot.com

Alan Howell
Medical Grade Essential Oils and Aromatics
www.shechina.co.uk

Avis Senior – BHSAI
Horse Riding – Choose your weapons

Thunderbrook
Organic and Natural Horse Feeds and
Educational Articles
www.thunderbrook.co.uk

Terry Shubrook
Kinesiology and Healing
www.terryshubrook.co.uk

The Masterson Method
www.mastersonmethod.com

Victoria Standen
Zoopharmocognosy / Animal Aromatics
www.harmonyhealingforanimals.co.uk

Liz Harris
McTimoney, Massage, Reiki
www.lizharris.co.uk

Suzanna Thomas
Centre for workshops and holistic horse care and products
www.spiritofthenaturalhorse.com

Henry Cumming
Horse Healing and Whispering
www.henrycumming.com

Kirsty Cooper
Horse Hair Jewellery
www.finedesignequinegifts.co.uk

Teresa Perrin
Bowen Therapy
www.teresaperrin.co.uk

Kay Emmerson
Sports Massage, Equine Aromatics, Kinesiology
www.equine-therapeutics.co.uk

Dawn Cox
Horse Rhythm Beads
www.angelhorse.co.uk

Helen Jacks - Hewett
McTimoney, Sports Massage
www.horse-back.co.uk

Rosie Hume
Masterson Method
Norfolk and North Suffolk
Tel: 07786 545977
Email: rosie3319@gmail.com

Lou Wilks
Masterson Method
www.naturallyhorse.co.uk

Julie Dexter
EMRT Bowen and Crystal Healing
www.bowenbalancing.co.uk

Emma Knowles
Veterinary Physiotherapy and Equine Touch
emma4et@hotmail.com
07921258752

www.theequinetouch.com

www.navp.co.uk

ABOUT THE AUTHOR

Holly has been working as a professional Animal Communicator and Therapist since 1999. She currently lives in Wales with her seven cats and three Arabian horses.

She is the Author of several books and courses on animal therapies. These are available throughout the UK as well as internationally.

She has a keen interest in natural behaviour and medicine as well as, psychological disorders in animals. A huge amount of her time is spent helping people to understand their animals. Aid in their recovery and create a better life for them.

Holly was one of the first Animal Communicators to teach workshops in England and is the Author of the first recognised Animal Communication Diploma in the UK.

Her accredited courses are available through Stonebridge College, links for which can be found on her website.

For information about Holly's other books please visit:

www.hollydavis.co.uk

Coming in 2015

Horsemanship - The Revelations

Horsemanship - Creating the Magic

Made in the USA
Charleston, SC
12 January 2015